LGBTQAI+ PHOBIA IN THE MENTAL HEALTH SYSTEM

By the survivors themselves

FOREWORD BY DR SARAH CARR

COMPLIED BY DOLLY SEN

EDITED BY DEBRA SHULKES
& DR CASSANDRA LOVELOCK

First published 2024

All rights reserved. This book or any portion thereof may not be reproduced or used in any manner whatsoever without the express written permission of the publisher.

The authors have asserted their right to be identified as the authors of this work in accordance with the Copyright, Designs and Patents Act 1988

British Library Cataloguing in Publication data: a catalogue record for this book is available from the British Library.

© Debra Shulkes, Dr Cassandra Lovelock and Dolly Sen

COVER DESIGN: Caroline Cardus

ISBN 978-1-7393589-2-1
Ebook ISBN 978-1-7393589-3-8

WWW.CUCKOONESTBOOKS.CO.UK

Funded by

Dedicated to the memory of the most wonderful, beautiful, kind and glorious Debra Shulkes (1975-2022)

CONTENTS

FOREWORD BY DR SARAH CARR

INTRODUCTION BY DOLLY SEN

QUEER HEADS MEET COLD HEARTS

1. Dolly Sen – *Queer in the Head*
   19

2. Julie McNamara – *Ready, Steady, Retreat*
   24

3. James Withey – *He's Your Friend*
   36

4. John-James Laidlow – *The Examination*
   43

5. O.S. – *Seeking an Autism Diagnosis as a Non-Boy*
   49

6. Lydia Rose – *Unbound*
   60

7. Artemisia – *How DID Affects Gender Transition*
   73

8. R.S. – *Queer Longing*
   84

9. Sophie Hoyle – *The Compartmentalisation of Care*
   95

10.   Alex Farine – *On the Surface*
108

BIS ARE QUEERS TOO

11.   Sean Burn – *Bi Not Bye*
113

12.   Ellie Page - *Out of Mind, Out of Sight*
126

WE KNOW THAT QUEERNESS IS NO LONGER SEEN AS A MENTAL ILLNESS BUT WE WILL STILL FUCK YOU OVER WITH A PERSONALITY DISORDER LABEL

13.   Artie Carden – *There's No Sense to be Made in the UK Mental Health System*
140

14.   LJ Cooper – *Diagnostic Dysphoria*
154

15.   Hattie Porter – *My Sense of Self, Or Your Sense of Me*
163

16.   Jo Doll – *That's Not My Name*
170

17.   Z Mennell – *There are Scratchy Woollen Jumpers Under My Skin*
179

THE MENTAL HEALTH SYSTEM IS HERE TO POLICE YOUR GENDER

18. Cal – *Closets and Revelations: a Madlesque Variety Show*
194

19. Katie Morison – *We're Used to It*
206

20. Luke 'Luca' Cockayne – *Only Women Get Jilted*
216

21. E.O. - *'Clinical Issue': How Pathologising Transness Forces Us Back into the Closet and Enables Abuse*
221

22. Z'ev Faith – *Beyond the Bonds of the Binary: Towards Queer/Trans/Mad Liberation*
227

23. Freida Blenkinslop - *Feminism: An Aid to Understanding Personal Abuse in a Societal Context*
238

OUR GROUP MESSAGE TO ANYONE HOLDING ELITIST OPINIONS (written by Dr Cassandra Lovelock)

"Peoples' stories are their own, in whatever form they have been put across in this book. For that reason, I beg you to take your elitist opinions and shove them up your ass. These books are not grammatically perfect, it has not softened itself for our readers, and we have not asked our authors to reshape themselves to fit into already formed constructs and narratives about mental health. This is not an academic book, though every academic should read it and weep."

FOREWORD - Dr Sarah Carr

Dolly Sen's artwork, a collecting tin labelled 'Help the Normals', positions those considered to be 'normal' as in need of charity. Now, in this remarkable book, Dolly and their collaborators share powerful accounts of what it's like to be considered 'abnormal' and in need of psychiatry. Free to express themselves as they choose, the authors tell stories of pain, trauma, resistance, and survival. Some use art to convey their experiences, while others write about their lives. They describe the horrors and absurdities of the psychiatric system and explore the journeys they have taken in becoming themselves. Their voices speak in many tones. In their uniqueness and diversity, they defy mundane normality.

RS explains that they are 'queer in the sense that I can't understand the straight logic of the normalised'. This resonated with me greatly, particularly as one whom psychiatry tried to 'straighten out' as a teenager, in a system defined by a logic that classifies and treats those who deviate from 'the norm.' I couldn't understand why I needed to be normalised. We know that in England aversion therapy was used to treat lesbian and bisexual women in a vain attempt to turn them into heterosexuals (Spandler & Carr, 2022).

In an interview for the Hall-Carpenter Oral History Archive at the British Library, 'Queercore' punk music pioneer Liz Naylor recalled her experiences in a juvenile psychiatric unit, where she was admitted for treatment in 1977:

'…so, they bundled me off to this horrible, low, flat, Sixties built unit in Macclesfield in the middle of a field next to Parkside Mental Hospital… it was like prison…I sort of sussed that I was in because I was gay…I just thought this is so weird I'm in this place. I felt perfectly normal and felt quite happy that I was gay now and was ready to go out in the world, but I was too young to do it, so they put me in there'.

What was normal for Liz was not normal for society, so along came psychiatry to set her straight. If you think of psychiatry's straightness, you may think of that cruel instrument of restraint, the 'straitjacket.' A 'strait' is a narrow passageway, constricted and tight, a place that can trap you. As several of those writing here attest, too many queer, trans and gender diverse people are still restrained and trapped by diagnostic labels, now slapped on through sleight of hand. 'Homosexuality' may no longer be classified as a mental illness but as long there's a 'Borderline Personality Disorder' diagnosis, we remain in danger of being pathologised, invalidated and marked with one of psychiatry's stickiest labels.

In resistance to the narrow confines of imposed normality and the damaging constraints of psychiatric discourse, contributor Z'ev Faith determines that 'I want to use my own words to describe my own narrative and experiences. I will not rely on an unbending narrative within the bounds of binary and segmented pathology.' Elsewhere the survivor researcher Jasna Russo has reminded us that powerful psychiatric mechanisms 'devalue not only our personal stories but also our very ability to understand and make meaning of our experiences on our own' so we must 'start to explore the meaning of our experiences beyond the explanations we have been given' (2016, p.62-63).

Finding our own languages and modes of expression are vital acts of liberation from the narrow straits of psychiatry. For too long queer, trans and gender diverse survivor voices have been silenced and pathologised, trapped in medical notes and clinical research. In this book they are free to sing.

Dr Sarah Carr FRSA, survivor researcher and Visiting Senior Research Fellow, Service User Research Enterprise, Department of Health Service and Population Research, Institute of Psychiatry, Psychology and Neuroscience, King's College London.

References

Russo, J. (2016) Towards our own framework, or reclaiming madness part two. In Russo, J. & Sweeney, A. (eds.) *Searching for a Rose Garden.* Monmouth: PCCS Books (pp.59-68).

Spandler, H. & Carr, S. (2022) Lesbian and bisexual women's experiences of aversion therapy in England. *History of the Human Sciences 35* (3-4). https://doi.org/10.1177/09526951211059422

INTRODUCTION – Dolly Sen

This book is part of a project funded by Unlimited and the Wellcome Collection which explores and challenges the narrative in existing mental health archives and libraries, and goes some way to ease the trauma of mental health system survivors having to fight for the truth.

The idea for this project has been floating around in my brain for years, ever since I helped Anna Sexton do her PhD around the mental health archives at the Wellcome Trust, and saw how little of the voice of the people who go through mental distress is in the archives, how the human being is lost, silenced, demonised by the professional voice.

Why should the people who've never visited a land be that country's prime historians? How can we tell our true stories when our words are seen as sickness? Most mental health archives and libraries, as they stand, have observable data of inobservable worlds. Having mental health lived experience filtered by mental health professionals, is like lions representing bird song in roars.

Apart from the lack of authentic voices, the representation of mental health in patient notes does not give a person the essence of their life or their right to beauty. I remember reading my mental health notes and not recognising the person they were describing. Do you know I do not have copyright of these notes, these words that are about me, that judge me ugly and cannot tell the truth about me? I cannot correct them either, because addressing any misrepresentations in patient notes could be deemed a sign of my sickness, it can never be deemed a sign of the sickness of the system. The horrible thing about it is we have to accept these ugly words and diagnoses and stay silent to ensure we get our benefits and other help. The ugly words seep through the whole system. I realise the system cannot save me despite the few decent people in it.

The hidden song from the perspective of the individual has been lost or never valued in the first place. This is particularly true for groups discriminated against in society who have also been the subject of institutionalised discrimination from psychiatry.

Psychiatry is not a mechanism that relieves mental distress, it polices what is socially sanctioned behaviour, and one of the things it gives the people that go through its system is a deep sense of shame that they were disgusting enough to be sensitive to trauma or the brutalisation of their situation in life.

Historically many identities have been judged as problematic, or labelled mad. E.g., women diagnosed with 'hysteria', when they stepped away from their 'feminine' roles. Black slaves were pathologised for wanting to escape and given the label of 'drapetomania'. Gay people were given shock treatments and nausea-inducing medication to 'cure' them of their homosexuality.

Psychiatry has caused great pain to generations of people, and there are not many places they can say this without being punished for it, or not taken seriously or believed. I applied for Unlimited with the hope I could deliver three books of the survivor voice relating to those marginalised lives under the name of Cuckoo's Nest Books. Whether you are a woman, a racialised person, or a LGBTQIA+ person in our society and mental health system, you feel like you don't belong and not permitted to tell your truth. We also decided to pay our writers to acknowledge their labour. Survivors are often asked to give up their stories to professionals, charities and others for free. I know when I have turned down unpaid work, some professionals have thought I was being 'difficult' because of my 'madness'. This has to stop. Survivors need to be paid for any work they do.

Luckily, with the help of my ever-lovely producer Caroline Cardus, we got the funding to deliver three performances and three books on the subjects of misogyny, LGBTQIA+ Phobia, and racism in the mental health system.

Despite their incredible talents and abilities to tell a much richer story than any psychiatrists could dream of, for some contributors it isn't safe to be out as a system survivor or critic - many people are publishing under a pen name. For those writing about their trauma for the first time, there was the concern that the process would be triggering or that for those who have been tormented by constant criticism all their lives, being edited would feel more of the same. When I first started to write professionally, the editing process was very difficult. I had been conditioned to see myself by both my upbringing and psychiatry as useless, worthless, a failure, and any suggestion of change was evidence of this. With time I learned to separate the editing process from the personal bullshit conditioning I had and see it as a way of improving my writing and grammar (I left school at 14). We were very aware of this possibility and tried to be as gentle as possible.

This project brought up many unexpected learning curves we need to build on. Separating the books into single issues was bound to have an influence on intersectionality, as Audre Lorde says 'we don't live single issue lives'. But for this project, lack of time meant a limited amount of authors, and most LGBTQIA+ people wanted to write for our LGBTQIA+ book, and most of those who experienced racialised discrimination wanted to write for the racism book, so the books have splintered slightly. The three books dialogue and complement each other, and it is recommended all three are read together.

This book is one place people can talk of how phobia, discrimination and around people's LGBTQAI+ identities affected their mental health and their time in the psychiatric services. LGBTQAI+ stands for Lesbian, Gay, Bisexual, Trans and Questioning or Queer, Asexual and Intersex plus.

A Stonewall (2018) study found:

- half of LGBTIQ+ people had experienced depression and three in five had experienced anxiety
- one in eight LGBTIQ+ people aged 18 to 24 had attempted to end their life
- almost half of trans people had thought about taking their life.
- Forty-one per cent of non-binary people said they harmed themselves in the last year compared to 20 per cent of LGBT women and 12 per cent of GBT men
- One in eight LGBT people (13 per cent) have experienced some form of unequal treatment from healthcare staff because they're LGBT.
- Almost one in four LGBT people (23 per cent) have witnessed discriminatory or negative remarks against LGBT people by healthcare staff. In the last year alone, six per cent of LGBT people – including 20 per cent of trans people – have witnessed these remarks.

Stonewall, 2018. LGBT in Britain: Health report.

Isolation, rejection, discrimination, abuse and inequality from family and society is not a recipe for beautiful mental health.

LGBTQIA+ people: ego-dystonic homosexuality was a psychiatric disorder in the DSM up until 1980; 'gender identity disorder' was in the DSM until 2013. The other corrupt catalogue – the International Classification of Diseases (ICD) – only removed homosexuality as a mental illness in 1992. Being trans was only removed from the ICD as a mental illness in 2019.

I am Queer in the head. What I have learned in my many years in the system is that psychiatry does not love Queerness. It has never loved me, and it has never loved the many generations of Queer people before me. It has institutionalised, lobotomised, castrated, over-medicated, aversion-therapied, pathologised, ECTed the head and electroshocked the genitals of people it has deemed sick, punishment pretending to be treatment.

As part of my research in the Wellcome's archives, I found information about aversion therapies in the 1950s and 60s. Aversion Therapy was a process where gay patients were exposed to sexualised images of people of the same sex, while simultaneously being subjected to emetic drugs to make them vomit and shit themselves. There is a voice in the archive, from the BBC Radio programme 'All in the Mind', of a man from Liverpool called Peter. He talks of being locked in a windowless cell and whilst he was shown pictures of naked men felt like he was being tortured when he was given an injection to induce vomiting and lack of bowel control. The whole thing terrified him, but he came out of the treatment still gay, which puzzled him because he said 'Nobody wanted to be straighter than me.'

It was mostly done to gay men, but some lesbians were inflicted with aversion therapy too.

The psychiatrist told my parents about me being a lesbian, and against my will, my mother signed a consent from for aversion therapy in the hospital. For the next six weeks I was given injections [to induce vomiting] and electric shocks when pictures of women came up on screen. I was made physically ill at the sight of women doing anything. For three months I felt terrible. It put me off women. I could not face being anywhere near them. What it didn't do was make me like men. (Gardiner, 2013: 62)

And some people wonder why some Queer people hate themselves.

Shame is a beautiful lesson to learn as a human being. It does wonders for the soul. It gifts you a loneliness that might break you. Let's electroshock – let's restrain them – let's carve away bits of their brain – but let's forget about love. From this arrogant and cruel standpoint, why are the stories of queer people written by people who hate them? I am talking about patient notes, case studies, conversations, clinical communications.

If LGBTQIA+ people are traumatised by how the world has treated them, the trauma deepens once it meets with psychiatry. Even if it no longer physically tortures people in a unique way, this institution that doesn't love them has way too much power over LGBTQAI+ people.

As of 2022, Conversion Therapy for trans people has still not been made illegal, where the aim is to 'repair' someone's gender identity by breaking them and causing them untold suffering. The other power it has is psychiatry's gatekeeping role is everywhere - access to benefits is impossible without 'medical evidence' and a psychiatrist decides whether people qualify for medical transition (e.g., access to hormones and other services). Gender Identity Clinic psychiatrists decide whether someone *is* trans and what the endpoint of their transition should be. Psychiatry and queerness or transness are all about compulsive heterosexuality and being gender-policed. In the book there are examples of psych education forcing people to perform traditional cisgender roles and compulsory heterosexuality as part of 'care'.

Psychiatry remains an incredibly conservative profession. There is still denial or contempt for queerness, non-binary identities, polyamorous lifestyles and asexuality - these parts of people's identities are routinely pathologised, usually labelled 'identity disturbance' to justify a personality disorder diagnosis. Despite it having almost no biological evidence of most mental health conditions, it professes to be the expert of what is in LGBTQIA+ people pants and hearts, and it will always be under the mantle that a straight orgasm is more righteous and preferable than a queer one. Any pain will be attributed to 'pathology' of a person's LGBTQIA+ identity, and not because of how they are treated by a clinically and religiously endorsed hatred. Unfortunately, within the LGBTQAI+ world hatred throws its spikes there too. There is a denial of asexuality in the LGBTQIA+ movement, which some of our writers talk about.

There is some invisibility of bi people in queer circles, and bi people have no space in psychiatry to explore that because they are pathologised there as well.

We live in the times of the TERFs (trans-exclusionary radical feminists), who seem to be waging an all-out war on eliminating trans and non-binary people, and are given way too many platforms to do this.

Because there is this underlying derision and conceit about around sexuality and gender in our society, people are not supported or even tolerated for being unsure and experimenting with queerness, gender and polyamory. Almost everyone LGBTQAI+ travels the mental health system in silence and secrecy, only allowed to speak with the silencer's words or define themselves within a terminology of revulsion and loathing. They are not given the right to use their own language or expression to describe their experience and lives. This book gives them some space to tell their truth.

This book shares stories of pain, but also features people's unsmotherable spirit, humour, community, art, rage, and brilliance. The contributors answer back, exceed, mock and fight for the end of the system that doesn't want them to exist. We exist. Beautifully.

QUEER HEADS MEET COLD HEARTS

QUEER IN THE HEAD – Dolly Sen

I was already confused about gender before I even knew what sexuality was. Between my ears and in my heart, I never felt like a girl, but I didn't feel like a boy either. Years of bewilderment followed. I understood later that I am non-binary. When I was young, however, bewilderment stepped aside to make room for the brutalisation, the pain, the violence, the horror of existing in an extremely abusive household, and experiencing other things like poverty and racism.

When I look back on my young gender-non-conforming self, I want to stress that I did not choose to feel that way; I *was* that way. There are some people who think it is a choice, but who would choose to feel outside of the rest of the world, life a painful performance in a body that does not belong to you. I did not play with toys aimed at girls, had no interest in make-up, dresses or anything like that growing up. It does puzzle me today to hear transphobic people think we don't actually exist, or that they believe they have the right to say who should and shouldn't exist. They would like us not to live but we do. There are powerful sectors of this world who want a genocide of trans and non-binary people. This is not an academic point. My friend, Andrea Waddell, was murdered in 2010 for being a trans woman. How could anyone ever think that is right?

Things then got even more painful and complicated for me once sexuality become part of my teenage experience. I grew up in a strict Christian family where TV and reading material were monitored. I didn't know anything about gay people at all.

I remember my dad insulting Billie Jean King, the lesbian tennis player, and using derogatory terms to describe her. I had no idea what she had done 'wrong'. I had crushes on Donny Osmond AND the Bionic Woman as a kid.

As I got older, I had more crushes on girls than boys. When I reached puberty, I felt a sexual attraction to women. I knew what a lesbian was at that point, but I didn't want to be one. *Fuck the idea that being gay is a lifestyle choice.* There is no choice at all. The pressure to be straight is enormous. What young person welcomes disappointment – or an even worse reaction – from parents who want the straight wedding and 2.4 kids for their child?

Compulsory Hetrolife and Love

Compulsory heterosexuality is the idea that heterosexuality is the norm assumed and enforced by society. I was a teenager in the 1980s, the decade Margaret Thatcher introduced Section 28. The law is named after Section 28 of the Local Government Act 1988. Enacted on 24 May 1988, the amendment stated that a local authority "shall not intentionally promote homosexuality or publish material with the intention of promoting homosexuality.

This meant that I didn't see any people who were similar to me, in sexuality, gender identity, or skin colour, and I didn't have any role models. **Heterosexuality was compulsory**. The world was heteronormative. Heteronormativity is the world view that heterosexuality is the preferred and privileged sexual orientation.

At a time when I needed to make sense of my feelings and sexuality, I was instead offered repression, depression, and self-hatred.

Compulsory cis-heterosexuality is not a gun-to-the-head sort of coercion and oppression, more of a gun to the heart that most straight people don't see or choose to ignore. They don't see the economic, social, legal, political and medical punishment for being anything other than straight or cisgender.

I tried desperately to be straight. I mixed up thinking a man was handsome with thinking I fancied them. When I kissed boys as a teenager, I felt no pleasure or connection – but it was what I was supposed to do to fit in, to not be treated badly, to not be murdered by my dad. It's what kept me alive and with a roof over my head. I have no doubt that I would be dead or homeless if I came out to my dad at that point.

The Hetero Mental Health System

So much was at play in my life back then, including childhood adversity. But my sense of disconnection and being hated by a homophobic world contributed to the psychotic condition I developed, aged 14. Why didn't services ever explore the intersecting forms of bigotry being directed at me?

The racism, misogyny, homophobia and transphobia became part of the shitty committee of my voices and paranoia that told me I was not good enough, that there was something wrong with me. I now understand mental health services to be a cog in a bigger system. The tyranny of normality is an autocracy of control.

I was too unwell to work until I was in my 30s. I also kept my sexuality a secret until then. Once I did come out, I received homophobia as part of my treatment plan from the mental health system; it often came in small but toxic ways.

After I had broken up with a girlfriend, a nurse said to me, "You're better off with a man anyway." Another nurse said I was going to hell for being gay. Even if staff were not overtly homophobic, they always assumed I was straight. Being LGBTQAI+ in this world can be traumatising but that distress is utterly disregarded in the mental health system. It doesn't want to heal trauma; it merely adds to it.

If I didn't know whether a mental health professional was homophobic or not, that part of myself was not brought up because I didn't feel safe. Besides, it was not brought up regardless. This had far-reaching and quietly devastating consequences. How to talk about painful things around homophobia? In the mid-noughties, I was sat out a pub in Peckham, London, holding a woman's hand when suddenly a shot rang out. Once the confusion settled, we saw a gaping hole in the pub window just above our heads. It was caused by a bullet. The police came quickly but the youths had disappeared. Our accounts were recorded by the police and I went home, deeply shaken.

It only dawned on me later that me and the woman I was holding hands with were the target. What was the awful thing we were doing that warranted an attempt on our lives? Holding hands? Who could I talk to about what happened? I couldn't with my mental health team. I feared homophobia. I feared the agony of their loathing being heaped onto suffering a hate crime. I stayed silent whilst feeling destroyed inside. Every Queer person on the planet understands how deep this loneliness can be.

I am proud to be Queer. I am unashamedly Queer, and I know psychiatry hates that. Most mental health professionals I have talked to about heteronormativity, don't even know what that means, let alone how it manifests in their work.

If a Queer person is looking for some kind of love or kindness from mental health services, they are going to be heartbroken every time. There are millions of broken hearts thanks to the mental health system. Even though being gay is no longer an official mental illness, there are still professionals who refuse to acknowledge that, or those who believe being gay is an unnatural offence. When will they realise that hatred, abuse, and neglect are the disorders and ugly reactions? In the meantime, I am Queer, and Queer in the head at that, I have heart to be proud of, and until the mental health system addresses its multiplicity of oppressions, us Queer people will always have more heart than they will ever have.

We have to be the singer and the song for those who have forgotten how to sing and those who have been silenced forever. Let the quiet birds sing. One day we will drown out the hunters. We have to. I am tired of seeing the pile of bodies of the dead.

2

READY, STEADY, RETREAT! – Julie McNamara

1.

On enquiring why I was now locked into a revolving door of shrinks and therapists, I was told I was 'experiencing a homosexual retreat'. It was 1980, I thought maybe I'd missed something? My immediate reaction was to sign up for that very retreat, as there might be a small chance of getting laid, or better still, finding somebody I could talk to. On further enquiry, I discovered that they objected to my 'masculine attire'. Through their lenses I looked 'a bit butch' and butch, my friends, was not a good thing, according to the gender police inside the mental health system. I look back and wonder at the treatment I received.

Where do we learn the chutzpah, the dare-devilry to flaunt our freak flag so young? Was it at my mother's knee, the very Queen of the Mersey, whom I loved with a passion? She flattered Gina Lollobrigida, dressed like a fifties film star, in high femme glamour with sultry looks and a mind full of mischief. I was her gatekeeper, always on guard. She called me her 'little soldier' and that is exactly what I became. I sense that template was also my undoing. There's little call for old soldiers among the alpha femmes I fall for.

There are many scenes in my early life missing from memory. Your guess is as good as mine. I was a bright child. 'Sharp as a tack', they said. But there were too many sharps in our house. I am still afraid of knives. Some things don't bear thinking of.

My earliest memory was before I was walking. They called me Nancy Shufflebottom because I propelled my body backwards on my bum, kicking out with one leg to launch myself way beyond their reach. I was over two years old when I first began to walk. When I finally made it onto my feet, I ran hell for leather out of there.

I first left home when I was three and a half. Still wearing reins with a little lamb on the front. I'd seen all these coloured balls on string floating outside the house down the road. We'd passed it on the way in. I left my mother emptying the car boot of shopping and ducked out the front gate to follow the floating balls. I'd never seen balloons before. I followed all these little people queuing at the garden gate, holding onto their respective grown-ups to join what I learned afterwards was a party. Nobody noticed I'd come alone, so I walked straight in. Brazen. I had never seen a table so laden with food. They had every type of cake you could dream up, with butter cream, sprinkles and chocolate bits, sherbet bits, angel delight and failed blancmange. I'd had jelly before, so I gave that a miss and proceeded to work my way down the table, hoovering everything in sight. I'm not sure I made it to the bottom of that table before I threw up across their lovely lino floor. A tall woman with long grey hair and a generous bosom scooped me up into her lap, turning her hair into a topknot with a flick of her hand, as she popped me between her magnificent breasts. And that's where it all began. Right there: the love of perfumed creatures with voluptuous, delicious curves, and the terrible fear that everyone else is having a party without me.

I sank deeper into her bosom, where the world calmed as a sensory overload of shrieking children and way too much sugar began to recede. I don't know which was the greatest pleasure in truth. My saviour's magnificent breasts or those magical colourful balloons?

But the stain I left on the lino was a stain on my character. I know I hadn't been a legitimate guest at the party, but I had been found wanting. I was never asked back. Too much too soon?

2.

Will I tell what I saw? Some things are best left unsaid.

Domestic violence sounds way too cuddly, if you ask me. But nobody ever did.

I was twelve when social workers first got involved. Fifteen when they gave us free memberships to the local Youth Club. We needed creative distractions, a social life beyond the pressure cooker that had become our home. Nineteen when they sent me to my first psychiatrist. She was very remote emotionally with very small breasts that offered nothing in the way of feeding. We didn't get on. Then came the round of clinics, outpatients' services and a couple of spells inside. I was terrified of madness. I'd seen my father's up close and had heard desperate stories of his father before him, who'd tortured his children, hanging them up by their braces on the old cottage beams and beating their bare feet with a cudgel. What kind of human does these things? Ours. Our kind. That is what we do inside the festering walls of our home. We beat the living daylights out of you, if you fail to toe the line. 'Do as I say, not as I do.'

'It was an accident; not an incident...' my father insisted when the police were called, and later, when anybody referred to past events, where he was found in dubious states of disarray.

There was the incident with the iron bar, no, that was an accident. There was his long night in a manhole in the road, could've been a dreadful accident that one, but it was downplayed.

There was the first and last unsupervised access visit he ever had, when we three kids were almost drowned at Hilbre Island, costing the emergency services a rescue helicopter, a lifeboat and a Land Rover ride to shore. That was a hideous mistake involving a deflated dinghy fixed up with flesh-coloured airstrip plasters. But that was yet another 'accident; no resemblance whatsoever to an incident.' I took that mantra of his for my own, as a universal explanation and get-out-of-hell card as I grew up. I look back at a wide range of catastrophic events that rolled out seamlessly without respite and can only say, 'It was an accident, not an incident…'

One particularly boring afternoon, the police were called to a disturbance on our street. I'd been wearing his clothes out in public, shuffling across the road, stopping the traffic. I wasn't sure what had offended them more: that a ten-year-old female-sexed child could pass for their father, or that that same child felt perfectly at home controlling traffic on a main road. The nosy neighbour, Sadie Bowie, had called the police first and then had my mother on the phone, barking at her to 'get the kids in, there's some weird bloke on the street.'

I loved my father's trilby. It was navy blue, with a matching tie that had a lighter blue stripe running through it. I loved the dark blue hand-me-down Crombie coat that we'd inherited, with its wee red handkerchief in the pocket, which I discovered was the red silk lining of the coat pulled through the pocket for display. I fancied myself in those clothes. There was no question I cut a dash in that get-up although his coat was too heavy for my puny shoulders. I was the runt of the litter back then. We can all dream big, apart from the police, who do not take to dreamers. My father was reprimanded. I took a beating with his belt. It must have been beyond bad; I got the buckle end.

3.

Too many deaths in my early twenties and I went spectacularly mad with grief. In a fit of pique with the world and all its misery, I swallowed a handful of acid tabs and flew off the bridge. Well, that was the intention. I'd always wanted to fly since I was a very young super hero. In actuality I flew off the bed and hit the wardrobe, wrecking the landlord's property and remaining stuck in and out of some drug-induced psychosis for months.

I vividly recall a spiritual journey in which I was called upon to fight and fuck with the devil himself. I swept through the cauliflower of my brain along canals of diarrhoea, trying to keep the tidal wave of past griefs from consuming me. I literally swept my brain clean, until finally I was drawn towards the light, surrounded by music and invited to join a group of kindly-looking women sitting in a circle. It's a wake-up call when you find the tambourine under your seat. The inner circle of goddesses has turned into the drab remains of the inpatients' music group.

It's the process of ritual humiliation that is so degrading when you are sectioned under the Mental Health Act here in the disunited Kingdom. The saccharine smiles and reassurances as they remove your status and sign away your right to drive your own recovery.

We do know when we've lost the plot, when we can no longer sleep at all at night, and we are forced to face the long grey days growing greyer in the soul.

'There is a pleasure sure in being mad that none but mad men know' but honestly, I can rarely find much joy in mine.

All pleasure in reading disappears. Words slip over the edge of the page. Everybody else seems to be moving very slowly and I can find no rest. Sleepless nights turn into days, then weeks, until gradually any sense of logic disappears. Or I find my own logic, which makes no sense to anyone outside my framing of the world.

Whose lenses are we required to peer through and collude with, when life is re-framed for us inside the acute ward of the local mental health service? I began to think I was lost inside a Hall of Mirrors at Blackpool Pier when I was required to spend some time detoxing from my ridiculous overdose of Lucy in the Sky with Diamonds.

Association time in the dayroom was a peculiar re-run of *Whatever happened to Baby Jane?* but without the Wardrobe and Make-up Department. Although to be fair, the nursing team always had a plethora of baby pink lipsticks and hideous dresses that had become the order of the day, all recommended by the nursing staff who were encouraging us to 'dress appropriately'. 'Just smile.' 'Go on, toe the line and you'll get out quicker...' It became a grotesque beauty parade for the staff and a distorted parody of gender roles prescribed by the consultant psychiatrist in charge. I found it harder and harder to play by their rules.

I remember Cara being cruelly stripped of her father's fabulous Sunday suit, which she wore to remain close to him, that smell of him, from the day after he died. She looked so suave in that suit. She could style it out, and she would have done, if she'd ever been allowed to ride that visceral storm of chronic sorrow after losing him. But they brutalised her battered heart, stripped her of the offending garments in a four-point restraint, they disposed of the suit and her dignity as they jabbed her, into her bare arse.

It makes me mad angry to think of that: the destruction of a perfectly good suit and the annihilation of someone's soul, to bend them out of shape to fit some image of femininity, the culture of the institution and the norms of the day. It always reminds me of the final words in the last shot of *The Hunchback of Notre Dame* when the camera closes in on Quasimodo, who's now sitting in the heights with a gargoyle: 'Why was I not made of stone like thee?'

There were at least three of us swapping stories of our homosexual retreats. Ana had been in the army. She was full of horror stories of the aversion therapy they'd subjected her to under the guise of treatment. It was all experimental in the early '80s. They were trying a scattergun approach, to see what would have the desired effect. They'd shown Ana porn images from magazines made for straight men with a penchant for vulvas. She recalled the oddest images of women's intimate body parts splayed open like raw meat. These cuties were a long way away from Dr Quant's presentations of 'Viva La Vulva!'. Ana described in graphic detail how the military nursing staff attached electrodes to her labia to give her shocks every time she showed any signs of arousal while looking at the train wreckage of images before her. She had us all entertained with her grimaces and gurning just recalling the state of those porn shots. They didn't get much joy out of their torture. And her feedback on arrival at the mental health unit where she'd been deposited after a dishonourable discharge was brief and to the point: 'It was a bloody waste of MoD funds. I'm still a dyke. No change there, but I did get addicted to fast pulse vibrators.'

They were supplied by Ann Summers back in the day. 'And thankfully,' she reported enthusiastically, 'it's never put me off women, but I'm not too partial to red meat these days.'

30

4.

I wonder how many therapists or shrinks I have known and loved in my life. Well, to be clear, not the bio blokes, it's all the women. Does that make me Queer? Gender dysphoric? Because I am 'more man than woman' as the shopkeeper described me to my blind friend, who'd quite rightly asked why the police had chosen to pick on me, out of all the people to choose from, shoplifting in the freezer aisle?

Should I give a fuck how others see me? I like being a Tomboy. That's what my mother called me. My father had a less glamorous description and wrote me off as 'a split-arsed mechanic'. It meant he would paint my entire room blue, including the bed, because he'd always wanted a son. I narrowly missed being christened Kevin when my father was drunk at the baptism. Still, it meant he would teach me to drive a car across Morpeth dock, where there were just three bollards between me and the bottom of the river Mersey. Were we playing Russian Roulette? It also meant he would teach me to row the rescue dinghy, to skull from the stern, to manage a marine engine at twelve.

I learned early that people write their disappointment across our bodies as well as our lives. And no parent is ever given a job description, which seems remiss to me. We have to hold a dog licence to keep a four-legged friend. Wouldn't it be sensible to teach parenting skills somewhere along the way.

Queer was a term of abuse on the streets back home in Birkenhead. Queer bashing was a gladiator sport. Still is. Some things don't change, no matter how we shake up gender roles and boldly re-frame our identities.

The worst basting was at the hands of a squaddie returning from the Falklands in 1982. I'd left home for pastures new, seeking a wider world and mischief. I have no doubt he'd suffered on his first visit to the Falklands. Nobody gets out of a war unscathed. He assaulted six women in a row at *Whispers*, a Gay night club in Nottingham centre, where he'd wandered in looking for late drinks and loose women. Neither were available at the time he dropped by to leave his calling card and I became acquainted with his hefty boots.

So, when people embrace the word Queer as an academic identifier for disrupting the trend of heteronormative thinking, I wonder if those same people have felt the annihilating pain of prejudice? Have they too met those hefty boots and been called to defend their very being in the world? Their right to be alive? Somehow, I doubt it.

But back to the shrinks. When your therapist starts wearing perfume you need to read the signs. When they start with make-up that seems freshly applied before your session at the close of the day, watch out. Read the red flag.

I have swapped cautionary tales with fellow survivors of the services, my own and others' howlers that have become reminders to us, that we are all of us, only human. That regardless of the power imbalance, the obviously inappropriate setting for lust, the professional boundaries between therapist and patient have been crossed and crossed again.

I can only hint at the mischief I have made. Knowing full well it was a breach of the psychotherapeutic relationship.

Part of the therapeutic process is to create attachment. There's a falling in love, which is a madness in and of itself. It's a classic textbook process, the patient is destined, all too often to fall in love with their shrink. But it's verboten for that same shrink to respond. Taboo. A no-no. Career suicide. And I can provide some messy examples to prove it's rarely equal and seldom based on mutual respect.

What if your therapist slips over the edge? I mean quite literally. I was in therapy with a fabulous woman who I was immediately attracted to. Without wanting to sound completely delusional, I have to say she was instantly attracted to me. Call it chemistry, call it madness. You take your pick.

She was training in psychosynthesis and was an expert in massage, so we'd sit and unpick the pains of the past and then she'd invite me to slip out of my clothes and climb onto her table. Yes, this one had absolutely no understanding of boundaries, professional or otherwise. And I knew it.

I arrived at a session one fine summer's day and she'd ramped up the code a notch. Her therapeutic surgery was filled with aromatic oils and the usual massage treatment ephemera. There were scented candles swimming in the middle of an oil-filled vessel; the scent of magnolia, sandalwood and ylang ylang filled the air.

The room was cloying with pungent oils vying for attention and she smelled of something unfamiliar. Deodorant? Fancy perfume? Hair products? I have no clue. I am a no-frills frolic, so this was never going to work.

I walked into the treatment room for what turned out to be our last session. The curtains were closed and there was little air in the room, now filled with the sound of whales calling from the distance. That's the wet fishy ones, not the Eisteddfod. We talked for a while, but I felt jittery as she was wearing make-up and that was a first. We reached the close of the fifty-minutes 'talking treatment'. Why is the therapeutic hour only fifty minutes? That's disingenuous daylight robbery and a challenge to anyone's orientation in time and space. But I digress.

Let's set aside the chit-chat, trawling over the trauma. Who's got the energy in these hideous 'post-pandemic' days? It was all about the touch, her touch. She had great hands back then, before that last hoorah. I was, I have to admit, completely thrown by the fleeting sight of a ladder in her tights. I was both shocked that she was imperfect, potentially slovenly, and horrified at the hologram of her I'd constructed. I remember climbing onto the massage table, thinking all was not well. Something was irreparably broken; she was sullied and I would never view her in the same way again. All for a bloody ladder in her tights? Seems harsh, even now, all these years after the incident that most certainly was NOT an accident.

She had always been very skilled at deep tissue massage, but that afternoon her touch grew lighter, softer and less focused until finally she slipped down my well-oiled legs and hit the floor with a thud. I took a look over my left shoulder and she was lying face down on her belly, out cold.

I got off the table sharpish and put some clothes on. I knew how this might look should anyone find us like this, and it was me they'd come for.

I drew the curtains, opened a window and let some air in. Lifted her carefully by the underarms, dragged her over to the open window and propped her sitting upright against the wall. I poured her a glass of water from the jug she kept for post-massage revivals, blew out the pungent candles and let the world back in. The mournful whale sounds had moved on and there was a new track filling the room with sounds of the panpipes from Camden market.

She came to with the cold air and asked what'd happened. I pointed to the candles, the oils and the window. 'It was too hot in here. You fainted.'

'There is nothing wrong with my practice,' she said as her miserable face began to sag with spite. 'It is your negative energy. You have a very powerful energy around you. And that'll be £60 for today's session…'

'£60?' I could not conceal my outrage as I swept out of the door. 'I'll send you my invoice.'

And that is the true reason why Vinegar Tits sacked me, at a particularly devastating moment in my life, when the world was turned to hell in a handcart and I was under siege.

3

HE'S YOUR FRIEND - James Withey

      I'm in bloody psychiatric hospital. I'm on five-fucking-minute suicide watch.

I have my own room, but it's taken five hours to get me the key. It's not exactly luxury; in fact, think the exact opposite of luxury, no, go even beyond opposite and you'll get this room.

The bin has been set on fire by previous occupants, so the lid is black and stinks. The window only opens a few inches to stop you running out, I guess, but even if you were able to squeeze through, you would be trapped in a sort of atrium with dead plants. The bed is bolted to the floor for some reason; maybe in case you wanted to dismantle it and make makeshift gallows. Who the hell knows? They've taken my shoelaces away along with all my plastic bags, but have left all the drawing pins on the corkboard. I point this out to the nurse who's smiling in the doorway, and she keeps smiling and takes them away. What the hell is this? Do I have to do my own frigging risk assessment?

There is a sink sort of moulded to the wardrobe, and you have to wait for about five minutes to get any water. The door is wooden with a window in it. From the outside, the nurses can open the slats in the window and peer at me. They do this every five minutes for the first few days. At night, I'm woken up at regular intervals by the noise of the sliding window and a torch in my eyes. 'No, he's not dead, that's good,' I suppose they mutter to themselves.

I'm ill, obviously. I'm suicidal, which I guess counts as pretty ill. And I'm terrified. It's an all-male ward and I feel like I shouldn't be here. As a gay man maybe I should be on the female ward? I don't know. There are shouts from the hallway: one man screams, 'My head, my head.' Another man, who I meet on my way to the shower, tells me in extreme detail how he wants to scoop out another patient's brain with a plastic fork.

The other men are watching football in the TV room. I hide in my room because as well as not being myself, I am not one of them. I was never one of them; not at school when everyone wanted to play five a side, not at university when everyone wanted to watch rugby, not in the pub where the other men are leering at women.

I'm not made for this. I like art and books and theatre and writing and beach walks and flowers and foreign cinema. I don't like watching sport and talking about how to kill the other patients with synthetic modulable cutlery.

I'm looking for a sign that the ward staff promote diversity: give me some rainbow flags, a poster of a gay couple on the wall selling antidepressants, hell, anything at this point to make me feel safer. But there is nothing. And I feel scared.

In the occupational therapy group the next day, we have to go round and tell each other what we miss about our life 'outside'.

One man says his girlfriend, another his children, a third having a beer and then it comes to me.

I want to say, 'I miss my husband and my cat and my books. I miss watching programmes about choosing wedding dresses, and feeling safe. I miss looking at interior design pages on Pinterest and browsing eBay for studio pottery.' I say, 'pass.' which we're allowed to say. 'Pass' seems the safest thing to say. The occupational therapist smiles at me with a 'maybe next time' kind of look. I want to say, 'If I'm here next time, I would like to be in a coffin.'

I glance round at the other men; who can tell what they think? Will they come and punch me if I say I'm gay? Will they all come at me with plastic forks tucked into their boxers and gouge my eyes out for being a fag?

It's too risky. Being here is supposed to be saving my life and I feel that my life is more at risk. OK, so no one has threatened me, but somehow it's the not knowing that makes me feel worse.

What if I tell people and they seem to be fine but afterwards they all get together to stab me in my bed whilst I'm asleep? What if they initially come and hug me and tell me that they embrace all genders and sexualities but really they're part of a neo-fascist homophobic prison gang that has infiltrated my local psychiatric hospital? If I can end up here, if I've reached the point where I want to walk in front of a lorry and kill myself, then anything is possible.

I admit my mind is not exactly thinking clearly. I guess that comes as standard here, but still the image of the other patients coming towards me dressed as mummies, with pitchforks in their hands and glazed eyes, makes me shudder.

I don't want it to be like this. I don't want the ward to be like *One Flew Over the Cuckoo's Nest.* I don't want to see stereotypes of mental illness.

I want it to be filled with, well... I suppose I want it to be filled with people like me and with nice compassionate nurses and friendly catering staff. I don't want to hear the cleaners shouting to each other, 'They've gone and blocked the bloody toilets again.' They. 'They.' It's the 'they' that stings.

My first review is with a male psychiatrist in his office. He sits behind his desk. I sit on the other side, with a nurse who's half advocate and half security guard.
 'Yes, so how have you been?'
Terrified, I want to say. Scared of being killed, scared of dying, scared of not dying. Scared of being a gay patient in a straight male patient world.
 'And your medication?'
 'Yes.'
 'Are you taking your medication?'
 'Yes.'
 'And you've been out for an accompanied walk to the shop?'
 'Yes.'
 'And you've been to a therapy group?'
 'Yes.
 'And, yes, and this umm...Patrick, yes, you've seen him, have you?'
 'Yes.'
 'Yes, he's your friend, isn't he?'
 'My friend?'
 'Yes.'
 'No.'
 'No?'
 'No.'
 'He's not your friend?'' No, he's not my friend.'
 'No?'
 'No.'
 'Then who is he?'
 'Husband. He's my husband.'
 'Your husband?' He looks at me and shifts in his large leather seat, trying to disguise his disgust.

'Yes. He's my husband.'

I can see him wrestling with his morality versus his professional obligations. Which way should he go? Should he tell me what an evil sinner I am and that being gay is one-way ticket to eternal damnation or should he pretend?

I think about this man. I suddenly hate this man. I mean, I really hate him. I want to punch him in the head. I want to, I want to scoop his brain out with a plastic fork.
I imagine him at home, with a dutiful wife, and him, in his office pretending to be examining the latest psychiatric journal on how to deal with depressed gay men, but instead looking at porn as she cooks his dinner.

Suddenly, I feel like a nothing. I shrink as he gets bigger behind his desk. He looms over me with his glasses and his qualifications and his training and his power and his huge fucking salary.

I can feel the nurse beside me, also uncomfortable, but they say nothing. Not a thing. They're under his power too. Don't speak up in front of the psychiatrist, don't make a scene, think of that promotion you want, think about how difficult he could make your life. Don't speak up for this man.

I want to shout at him, I want to call him out for his homophobia and for being a wanker. I want to push the desk so that it squashes him and then he dissolves like the witch in *The Wizard of Oz*.

We look at each other. There's no 'oh, I'm so sorry, of course, he's your husband' or 'please accept my apologies for the mistake.' He says nothing and I'm really, really trying to keep eye contact because as soon as I break it, he's won. I keep staring and he keeps staring.

'Should James still be on five-minute checks?' says the nurse eventually.

'Fifteen now,' he says, now unable to look at me.

I leave. I want to feel like I've held my power with him and that I've made a point, that I'm still here and fighting him and fighting depression and that he's not made me feel even more worthless than I already feel.

I go back to my room. I want to hate him more, but I hate myself more instead.

Despite years of counselling and bravery and talking to myself about internalised homophobia and understanding external homophobia, I feel worse. And then I feel worse because he wants me to feel worse and I start to spiral even more than I have already spiralled – which, you know, is pretty far down when you're in a psychiatric hospital.

I sink into the bed. He's won.

Hurt comes in lots of ways but the hurt when you're already hurt, hits deeper. The hurt that comes from not being seen cuts deeper than my self-harm does. And the hurt of being shut down by the people that are supposed to care always hits hardest.

Now, I am under the care of a man who doesn't acknowledge who I am, who sees me and my husband as something other. This man, who is supposed to be making me better, has made me worse, and I don't know what to do.

What's the point in being here if I'm not seen, not validated, not understood? The walls to my room, which felt flimsy, now feel like paper.

My mind, which already felt destroyed, now feels obliterated, and all because he couldn't say I have a husband. My certainties are all I have at the moment: my home, my cat, the things I love, but most of all, my husband, and he just brushed that one right away.

I can hear the *Daily Mail* brigade of middle England shouting, 'stop being a snowflake,' 'get yourself together,' 'don't be so sensitive.' I try and shout back. I try and shout at him whilst he reads his paper in the morning on the toilet, but I have no voice.

I have to leave, but like a hostage, I need to talk to the guards first. And, of course, asking to leave involves talking to the prick psychiatrist again.

I say I don't want to talk to him. I say I want to talk to someone else, not him, not this man playing dress-up as a psychiatrist. But there's no option. I have no option.

I walk into his office again. He talks about access to the community psychiatric team, about medication prescriptions before I leave, about how I'm going to get home and how safe I feel, about how to… something, something, something. I'm not listening because I hate him.

I lie to get out. I say that I no longer feel suicidal, that I'm much better, that everything is fine now. He buys it. The idiot. He says goodbye whilst looking down at his computer. I look at him.
This creature.
 'I'm going,' I say. 'I'm going to see my husband.'

And I leave.

4

THE EXAMINATION (PARTS 1-4) - John James Laidlow

PART 1: 1991

'That's not a boy's toy' interrupts a ginger-haired kid with dirty fingernails.

It is the first day of school and it isn't going well. The teacher has sent a letter to our parents in advance asking us to bring our favourite toy to share with our new friends. So now in my clammy little hands, I hold my favourite My Little Pony toy. It is a blue unicorn with a pink mane and tail, the finest in my collection. But not even the iridescent fairy wings that move when you push a button on its back impress the other children.

At first, I think it must just be the boys because boys don't ever like me, but now looking around I can see the girls wearing matching expressions, noses crinkled in disgust. Something is wrong with me.

PART 2: 2000

From my hospital bed I can see straight through a wide window looking out into the corridor. Busy nurses shuffle on by. Their uniforms consist of the same white starched material as the bed sheets that hold me firmly in place, evoking a mixture of safety and restraint.

I have been on the children's ward nearly a week now and it feels like forever. I'm not sure I know how to exist outside of these walls anymore.

Mum is sitting in a hard plastic chair beside my bed reading a celebrity gossip magazine she purchased downstairs in the League of Friends shop. She licks her index finger before aggressively flipping each page. She has other things to be getting on with and I can feel her urging the doctors to hurry up on their ward round.

I wish they would hurry too so I can roll over into a stupor of painkillers, fantasy novels and naps. When Mum is gone at night and it is just the sounds of the nurses moving about and cooing like doves, the rhythmic beeping of heart monitors in the near darkness, I feel the most content I have in years.

I start to worry again that I'm somehow making myself sick, so I can be in here, looked after and safe. After all the doctors can't find any reason for this pain that has me doubling over every few weeks and producing thick yellow bile like banana milkshake from both ends. Perhaps I'm just a hypochondriac trying to get out of school. I hate school. I hope they find something wrong today so that everyone will know this isn't all in my head.

As if on cue, a doctor in a long white coat appears, ready for his matinee performance. I haven't seen this one before. He is old, with grey hairs sprouting in patches and from every orifice. Glasses perch precariously on his nose.

Behind the star stands a supporting cast of nervous-looking students. They avoid eye contact with me when I try to read their faces. My mum puts down the magazine and looks up, a captive audience.

  'Now I've heard you're in quite a bit of pain.'

I nod.

'Well, I'm just going to do a quick examination to see if we can get to the bottom of this and...'

He leans in towards me and lowers his voice to an almost-whisper.

'I hope you don't mind but these students are going to observe. We'll pull the curtains round to give you *a bit* of privacy.'

I look over to my mum for reassurance and she matches my gaze. This time she nods on my behalf and I lay down flat.

'Okay then, I'll slip your pants down...' and in one swift motion, he pulls down my pants from under my hospital gown.

'... and then if you roll over to face your mum with your knees bent up towards your chest.'

I do as he says and reposition myself. My eyes meet Mum's again and I'm terrified she will break this stare, see that I have started to grow pubic hair. I feel nauseous and my cheeks start to flush.

The doctor mutters something to the student doctors that I cannot hear and they all crowd round to stare at my naked bum. I can hear the crinkle of latex gloves.

'Okay, this might feel a little bit uncomfortable,' he says as he parts my cheeks

PART 3: 2007

'Are you sure you're gay?'

I look up from the tissue I've been anxiously twisting in my hands. I was given it at the beginning of the assessment, but almost 45 minutes in, it now looks like some sort of hair braid or rope. I meet one of the nurse's eyes, the one that hasn't said much at all, and then look at the other nurse who asked the question.

In the small side-room of the Minor Injuries Unit where I once went after a bad fall from my bike, I sit struggling to form words, trying to convince them that I don't need the Crisis Team to come in every day again.

They both stare back intently, pens poised above their notepads, waiting for me to speak. This is the first time I have been open with a mental health professional or any real grown up about my sexuality, and I'm not sure if I've said something wrong. I want help so I'm being open about everything. Is this the way it's supposed to go?

We sit in awkward silence, all three of us, for a few moments longer before the nurse formally diagnoses me as 'acutely confused', based on my lack of response. He elaborates: 'It's just gay men don't have facial hair.'

I don't want to say that my beard grew in due to self-neglect even before it became a trend again so now I'm sticking with it out of ease.

'Yeah. I think so. Anyw—'

PART 4: 2012

'I heard you were bisexual.'

My heart lurches in my chest, and I feel my whole body jump slightly. I hadn't even noticed anyone at my door or had time to pause the nature documentary I'd put on to pass time till the next day. I look up to see a familiar disdain.

'Who did you hear that from?'

'People were talking about it in the living room.'

I hate this place - a 'supported living' home apparently. It feels more like a supported living death. A place for me to live out my days because I don't fit anywhere else. All I do is take my meds, sleep, and piss in my bedroom sink because I am too scared to go to the communal toilet. Now the other residents are gossiping about me too.

'Was it staff?'

'Doesn't matter… you got any porn?'

I can feel his eyes invading the privacy of my bedroom, scanning around, searching my few personal belongings for anything out of the ordinary, or possibly something worth taking when I'm not around. Why would I even have porn? It's not like I have a use for it anymore.

'No, sorry.' (Why am I apologising?)

He sneers, looking straight at me.

'It's satellites, you know.'

I pause, not sure where this is going:
'What is?'

'Satellites in space. They send signals into your brain to make you gay. They use to do it to me but they know I'm onto them now.'

I say nothing. There is nothing to say anymore.

***

When you enter the mental health system –when psychiatry is brought in to assess and evaluate your life and identity – everything is up for scrutiny and judgement. Too often the people working within these systems do not appreciate or even understand the varied and unique ways that each person may express their sexuality and/or gender. These facets of what makes you 'you' are also seen as part of your 'deviations from the norm', expressions of illness that need to be noted and pathologised, or sometimes even fixed.

Wider societal experiences reinforce these ideas and unfortunately we often internalise the constant judgement that something is wrong with us.

5

SEEKING AN AUTISM DIAGNOSIS AS A NON-BOY –
OS (pen name)

Long before I suspected being on the spectrum, I suspected I was not a girl. Not wholly, at least; the word had never felt full in my mouth. A child of the internet, I gained access to texts on gender theory and blogs written by trans people which led me to the steadfast conclusion, right in my early teens, that gender was not something that would be cut and dried for me. (Some, I fear, might read this and feel some kind of distrust or even terror; is it really that easy to be induced into the feeling that your body does not belong to you? Are a few entries on the internet all it takes to seduce your children into the enticing world of the trans community? Obviously not - the internet merely helped in giving me a voice for the feelings I could not reasonably word by myself.) Several years later, the internet was once again partially to thank for helping me come to a different, though not any less significant conclusion. In the years in between these experiences, the latter of which I will get to in a moment, my feelings surrounding my identity as a non-binary person only solidified, and I currently live as someone who is out to most of their community and is very certain of who they are and where they stand within their personal relationship with gender. The times of distress and questioning are long gone, though unfortunately they have been known to occasionally be replaced by anger and disappointment when said identity is questioned or threatened.

I first thought I could be autistic during my first year at university. A year after that, I decided to formally pursue a diagnosis and so headed to my university's mental health and neurodiversity support centre. At the time of this decision, the autism spectrum, and the idea that I could live somewhere within it, were still relatively new thoughts. I couldn't tell you with complete certainty what it is I sought by heading to my Uni's support centre. I suppose if I had to boil it down, I was looking for some acknowledgement of my lived experience. I was already well familiar with feeling alienated in part thanks to my queer identity, but I had always felt there was something else, something bigger, which made me oh-so-distinctly separate from everyone else. And for the first time in my life, I had found something which could prove to be an answer for this terrible, lonesome feeling, one I had learned to ignore over the years so as to not drive myself (and others around me) completely insane. (Later, as the autism diagnostic process went on, my reasons for seeking a diagnosis evolved, but I would still argue that my core objective was to find an explanation for my feelings of complete alienation from others, which I felt went way beyond the feelings of distance from others I had heard my peers describe.)

The very same day I made it to the support centre, I spoke with an autism specialist who, after a short chat and an even shorter form, had agreed it was possible I could have autism. I was put in contact with a local team, part of a larger, NHS-run programme.

This began a lengthy, year-long assessment process, all online as a result of the then-starting pandemic.

Though slow, the process was relatively smooth until I entered the final phases of assessment. I progressed from appointment to appointment, each advancing stage signifying, as I understood it, a higher likelihood of being diagnosed as autistic. I eventually got to the stage where I was to see a psychiatrist. Unlike the other specialists before her, this doctor asked questions which I thought were out of place, to say the least. She rarely if ever asked about pathology, for one; by this I mean some of the aspects of my life I sought answers on, and which I had been reasonably led to believe, could be indicators of autism: my extreme sensitivity to noise and other sensorial experiences; my rigidity of thought and blunt speech; my overwhelming feeling that others had been given a rule book which I was lacking (a feeling, which I later came to find, is word-for-word how a lot of neurodiverse people describe their feelings of displacement within a neurotypical world); and so forth. None of these concerns of mine, which I had raised earlier in the diagnostic process and which, as I understood it, were what had led me to be considered for a diagnosis in the first place, were approached in much depth.

Instead, the psychiatrist asked about my parents and whether or not they were together; if I had ever tried drugs, and if so, which ones; and when I had started my period.

When she did refer to my concerns, she was quick to dismiss them, almost as if looking to tick them off a list. For instance, I remember her asking me if I enjoyed going out to clubs and the like. When I said yes, but only under quite limited circumstances, in situations where I had control over the environment, prior knowledge of the music being played and the type of venue I would be entering, she was lightning-fast in brushing me off.

I even offered her an anecdote about how, after being tricked by a well-meaning friend, I had felt compelled to leave a club and stand outside with some noise-cancelling earbuds in order to recover from the unplanned circumstances, something which at the time I did not feel was that strange until a friend later observed that neurotypical people would usually have an easier time dealing with a similar scenario. (Which isn't to suggest that this happening in particular necessarily points to me being on the spectrum; but I certainly believed, and continue to believe, that sensitivities such as these were at the very least worth investigating.)

To the best I can recall, before being asked about my period, there was nothing which directly suggested my bodily functions were impacting my diagnostic process, though I did suspect this would be the case. I did not expect any of my assessors to consider whether I was anything other than a woman, and I never bothered to clarify. Though I am comfortable in my identity, I avoid putting myself in situations where sharing it could prove damaging to me.
Even prior to this experience, I feared there was nothing to be gained from clarifying I was non-binary with my assessment team; the discomfort of being potentially misgendered beat any possibility of being prodded on my identity, which often happens in my life when I dare correct someone on how they address me. Besides, my identity was not the subject of investigation here, my potential neurodiversity was. As historically speaking, several studies and personal accounts point to women (and those who are perceived as such) having a much harder time being diagnosed as autistic than men and instead being dismissed as having another condition, I figured any other gender identities would not fare much better in that regard.

My gender, as far I can recall, had never been directly asked of me throughout the diagnostic process. The only information sheet I filled in was back at the mental health centre, and even then, most of what I had to write pertained to the diagnosis. There was very little general information I can recall being requested other than my name. No matter, I thought; this doctor had looked at me and concluded I had periods, and to that extent, she wasn't wrong. I couldn't fault her any more than anyone else I am used to encountering in my day-to-day life. Though uncomfortable, I found the period question ultimately harmless. I did feel the need to clarify I did not identify as a woman, but afterwards, I was prepared to move on, chalking up the relevancy of my period to matters of physical development, a consideration I understand that is often made in autism assessments. Instead, I was vaguely probed on my identity, which I tried to skip past as smoothly and quickly as possible. I was asked how I had come to the conclusion that I was not a woman, a question which I was not in any way convinced was asked in relation to my diagnosis.

My true discomfort came later, however, after a handful of other meetings and the final decision reached by the assessment team, comprised of the psychiatrist I had met with as well as a handful of others, only some of whom I had talked with directly.

I was told what I feared and had learned to expect. In sum: I was able to engage in conversation and did not interrupt my interviewers to speak about any of my special interests. As such, the team had reached the conclusion that I was not autistic. Of course, the final verdict was more complex than this.

I was eventually emailed a 10+-page report explaining the assessment process as well as the reasons that led the team to conclude I did not meet enough criteria for autism spectrum disorder.

In theory, I would have been fine with this; I did not necessarily seek out an autism diagnosis specifically so much as I sought out an explanation, an answer to the myriad of things I felt had always gone unexplained about me that only the autistic umbrella had seemed able to shine a light on. The report that followed, however, was everything but illuminating. Of the multitude of questions I had posed and situations I presented throughout the assessment process, almost none were directly addressed in the report. Though I had (virtually) met with four different specialists, and spoken to a fifth over the phone, the report seemed to prioritise the meetings I had had with the psychiatrist, the shortest of the bunch.

A strange, itemised summary of my life was offered with a bunch of grammatical errors and many details either misinterpreted or plain wrong. For instance, the report said I had a family member working abroad; an extra cousin with an extra illness; and other larger errors I am still perhaps irrationally uncomfortable writing down, however insignificant they may actually be. This frustrated me – I was already disappointed in the result, believing the reasons given for the non-diagnosis were poor and incongruent with what I had been previously told. Still, I looked to the assessors' report for some explanation, some other possible answer for all the questions I felt were still hanging in the air.

Instead, my life's summary only got stranger. A section surrounding my 'development' had been typed out, where the following had been said of my identity: 'started research at an early age; she learnt it from books'. 'It', I can only assume, referred to my gender and orientation, which I briefly spoke of during the meeting with the psychiatrist. This was an awkward read, to say the least. I remember laughing with discomfort when I first came across this section of the report. From there, it only got worse.

What followed was a perplexing, confusing word soup, a strange arrangement of letters which vaguely approached the questions I had raised during my assessment period. It mentioned my sensory issues, but did not explain why they did or did not contribute to a diagnosis. It claimed I made good on behaving neurotypically, yet I also spoke in a confusing, disorganised manner at times and did not show an interest in the interviewer – some of the tell-tale signs that someone may be on the spectrum according to their own assessment criteria, as I understood them.

It incorrectly stated I had not shown a reaction when prompted about one of my special interests, when the opposite had happened: I had tried to (briefly) engage with the interviewer on the subject and got no response, and as I have learned over the years, that usually means it's time to move on with the conversation.

In sum, this report served as a strange, distressing game of telephone; it did little to alleviate any questions I may have had about whether or not I existed somewhere on the spectrum, and instead came to conclusions I had already come to not only expect, but fear: I was not autistic because I was... polite?

These standards were not set by myself and certainly informed by racism, classism, ableism and gender norms and a myriad of other things which render the notion of 'politeness' useless, anyway.

Other reasons given included the fact that I had maintained eye contact with interviewers throughout the screening process; I did not interrupt at inappropriate times; and I showed intelligence and creativity (how these work as impediments to an autism diagnosis, I do not know).

Almost all if not all of these behaviours were, of course, wholly conscious and calculated. Like many others who are on the spectrum, I had felt it was imperative to maintain an air of 'normalcy' and emulate the behaviour of those around me – a need I had spoken of early on in the assessment process, precisely to avoid it being thrown back at me later in the game.

I had told one of the people evaluating me that I was aware of the concept of masking, a phenomenon where autistic or otherwise neurodiverse people put on an act of sorts so as to integrate within their community and not feel the repercussions that often come with behaving in the ways that come naturally to them. I had been expressly assured that my comments were noted and that my ability to mask, were that what I was doing, would not be a deciding factor when it came to my diagnostic result.

At the end of the day, I cannot be sure what those deciding factors were – all I know is that many of the comments I heard towards the end of my assessment process, as well as the ones in my report, pointed to one thing: my perceived womanhood had almost immediately worked to write me off the autistic roster.

The conclusions of my report all pointed to a possible diagnosis of anxiety. This was despite my efforts to highlight my sensory issues and to repeat to my examiners almost ad nauseam that my extreme difficulty in social situations was NOT a source of anxiety, but one of distress – I was not scared of other people because interacting with others made me nervous, a valid experience but not the one I happened to have. Instead, I explained, I was nervous around people because they appeared to be nervous around me. My natural behaviour, I had learned, perplexed them in ways that surpassed the possibility of me just being a plain ol' weirdo.

In the end, the final report given to me by the assessment team not only proved incredibly distressing, but severely unhelpful. If not being diagnosed as autistic was in the cards for me, so be it; but I had hoped that were this the case, I would be offered a well-thought out, reasonable justification for the conclusion.

Instead, the several pages worth of pointers which I had shared as potential signs of my neurodiversity went unanswered and the report concluded with a suggestion that anxiety was the main culprit for my behaviour—something which is blatantly not the case, I would argue. Not only have I long been treated for that diagnosis but during the assessment itself I immediately attempted to clarify I did not believe it related to the points I presented. Ultimately, this pleading of mine was noted as uncooperative behaviour. The report stated that I appeared reluctant to speak about my anxiety due to discomfort with the topic.

I went so far as to request a new report be made to rectify the many things that either went unaddressed or were blatantly wrong in my report - in particular, my gender. I found it odd that it had been mentioned in the first place, but then it was described in my report for no discernible reason, serving only to make me uncomfortable.

The team was kind enough to hear my request, which I did truly appreciate, but unfortunately, what got back to me was, I felt, an equally rushed report with an added footnote that read something along the lines of 'we care/ we are understanding/we are accepting of your gender identity' - a very strange, uncomfortable addition that seemed to silently plead I stop making a fuss, because they do care about my identity, because identities matter now, they had been told.

It seemed my gender identity somehow got both included and disregarded within this experience. In the end, I was left with more questions than I had answers, and a tingling sense of discomfort in my stomach that any clarification I could hope to get about my suspected neurodiversity would not come soon from any set of supposed experts.

Ultimately, I understand the team was just doing what they thought best and were not actively trying to work against me or attempting to dismiss my concerns.

Nonetheless I did get the impression that I was meant to feel 'relieved' at my non-diagnosis, which is far from how I actually felt on reading the results. If I were asked how neurodiversity/autism assessment teams can avoid discriminating against and traumatising those seeking a diagnosis, I would say first of all they need to sincerely acknowledge and strongly keep in mind the medical/diagnostic bias and discrimination held against non-men.

Above all, they need to listen to the people they are assessing; by anecdotal evidence, I've found that more often than not people who seek out a diagnosis are already aware of these discrepancies and are fighting very hard to be heard.

On that note, it's important to remember that not everyone has access to the same information as professionals. It's crucial for people's well-being and adequate assessment that teams understand the complex and mutable nature of autism, which can manifest in many different ways across genders and other areas. Assessors need to continue their research and stay informed on these nuanced ways autism can present. If this were done, I believe more people would seek out a diagnosis and have a positive experience.

6

UNBOUND - Lydia Rose

Daily Survival

Nowadays, self-care has become a full-time job that I am fully and completely invested in. Knowing that both my life and sanity rest upon my ability to meet my every need with as much loving-kindness I can possibly muster, I immerse myself in a holistic routine filled with so much nurturance that even the most devout self-care guru would be impressed.

Mornings usually begin with a cup of tea and a journaling session to release the immediate surge of thoughts I wake up with. With an aching hand and a restless mind, I then take to my Yoga mat, directing my focus with breath, movement, affirmations and crystals.

Bouncing out of my block of flats in ragged sportswear, I march to the gym with beats blaring through hefty headphones and a backpack half my size weighing on my shoulders. Soon unburdened, I push my feet hard against a pool edge and launch into the depths of a chlorinated ocean. Like a lion treading through water, I swim with all my might, thrashing through the elements and dipping between two worlds. After proving my strength, I settle down in a sauna, where sweet aromas of lemongrass and jojoba hover in the air.

Led by purpose, I strut into a nearby library to cast spells across a screen. As fingers tap away storms of passion and anguish, I am rewarded with a satisfaction that fills right to the pit of my stomach.

For each concise point and smooth alliteration, synchronistic rhyme and artistic narration, pleasure rolls across my skin and dissipates into the space between myself and the person who may someday read my work.

Once my creativity has been spent, I head home to face the evening. On a good day, a vigorous dance is enough to shake out the threat of panic lurching through my fleshly being. Other times, chatting with a friend or family member brings me back to the reality of a safe and supportive life. But on those nights when my defences shut down and I can no longer fight off the surges of underlying trauma, I go through the usual drill of dialling a helpline. Crouching down in my box-sized bedroom, I hear a familiar ringtone repeat as I cling to any comfort that surrounds me; the softness of a lilac rug, the sparkle of lepidolite, the smell of lavender. I squeeze down hard against the intrusion of a flashback, until finally my call is answered.

Suddenly I am ejected from my suit of armour and drop into an abyss of blinding terror. My body a frozen shell, I fall further and further down the well of my subconscious. Overwhelmed by the sensation of asphyxiation, the pull of imminent death rises up my spine. As I tumble down and begin to accept my fate, a voice echoes out, flinging a phone cord into my awareness like a lifeline.

'Hello, how can I help?' a woman asks, and I hang tight to our connection.
'I'm having a panic attack and I need someone to talk to,' I squeak.
My rescuer begins by taking me through the procedural questions. The attention it requires to answer brings a welcome relief from the dark space threatening to consume me.
'What usually helps when you're feeling panicky?' she inquires, and I skim through all the coping methods I've developed over the months.

'Talking to someone,' I tell her. 'And breathing. Deep breathing.'.

'Ok, would you like to do some deep breathing with me?', she asks. I squeal yes, my grip threatening to slip. She outlines how she'll guide me through the exercise and I put all my faith into this kind stranger to bring me back to safety.

'Breathing in: 1, 2, 3, 4…' she slowly counts. I let her words direct my inhalation, as if breathing is the only task I ever need to do to stay alive. Oxygen floods through my nostrils and I close my eyes, filling myself with compassion.

'And breathe out: 1, 2, 3, 4…' My mouth squeezes into a tiny O to slow down the rush of air expelling from my lungs. I shiver and whimper, tears welling up as pain surfaces. My neck pulsates, remembering the rope that once severed my right to breathe freely.

'Breathing in: 1, 2, 3, 4…' she says again. I suck in as much air as humanly possible, hoovering up the atmosphere as if to gulp the stars.

'Breathing out: 1, 2, 3, 4…' As I release and soften, memories of my torture arise – though not from a regular perspective. Too horrifying for my neocortex to record, my near-death could only be witnessed out-of-body in fractures that bled through nightmares of the ritualistic scene. Naked, I hung upside-down trapped in a web of ropes tied to a wooden door; my struggle a non-consensual initiation into a cult that violates the sanctity of life.

'Breathing in: 1, 2, 3, 4…' my rescuer repeats. My diaphragm expands as I focus on the present moment and internally recite my affirmations; *I am free now. I got away. I survived. I'm alive.*

'And breathe out: 1, 2, 3, 4…' As I let go of my breath, despair floods upwards and I weep.

I weep as I remember his hypnotic voice and transfixing hands narrate my sexual enslavement; as her nose runs across her outstretched finger to add addiction to their suggestions.

I weep as I remember the three of us conversing in their garden before the ritual began, my confidence dimming as they lead me through a cunning indoctrination process to impose themselves as idols.

I weep for all the souls captured before me, who I imagine clawed their ghostly arms above the astroturf to warn me: *This is not a ménage à trois with two charming strangers from a dating app. This is a cult. A cult that traffics women.*
  'Breathing in: 1, 2, 3, 4…'
I am free now. Free to breathe. Free to move. Free to think. Free to live.

Pandora's Box

I am awoken in the early hours by a neck trapped in the past. Flailing in the dark, I reach up to feel each connective tissue brace against an onslaught my eyes no longer see. Accustomed to post-traumatic night terrors and somatic re-enactment, I soothe and thank my rigid neck for bravely bringing up the truth after a year of dissociation. With warmth from a water bottle and comfort from chamomile, I calm each tendon's grip between collar bone and jaw.

Too rattled to go back to sleep, my mind wanders through the months since I snapped out of self-delusion and reached out for help. All the numbers I'd dialled, all the hours explaining what I'd been through, all the waiting lists I'd been left to rot on…

A 3-month wait for an assessment and then a 3-month wait after the assessment to use their service; a 6-month wait for a *re-*assessment at another service because my trauma was too severe for the services I'd waited for; a 9-month wait on a waiting list for the waiting list, and then another 9-month wait once on the waiting list…

Under the refuge of a feather duvet, I recall all the times I've been let down by the public mental health system. Memories of the violence and abuse I've survived since childhood float through my mind and my sadness melts into the softness that surrounds me. Once liberated from my earlier abusers' hold, I reached out for support with the patterns of shame and anxiety I held onto after. Though most service providers I'd spoken to over the years seemed to genuinely care, there was never any help available. I was told there was not enough support to go around for all those unable to cope on their own, and I was doing too good a job of avoiding self-harm and suicidal ideation for the system to spare a hand.

When the spell of Stockholm Syndrome broke and the reality of cult abuse hit me like a train, I already knew the system I was up against. With the pandemic raging outside and my pockets tied by unemployment, it seemed impossible that I could find more support than hotlines for those experiencing severe mental distress. Caught in a sticky spot and quickly descending, I reached out to a cult information centre and through them a kindly woman named Mary saved me from my predicament.

Mary was a highly capable and deeply knowledgeable therapist who had dedicated her career to helping others like herself who had escaped cults. She was an elderly lady with a smile so gleeful it felt like we were two kids back in the sandpit, and we connected instantly through webcams. After significantly reducing her fee, Mary worked with me to address my trauma through an integrative mix of counselling and Eye Movement Desensitisation and Reprocessing (EMDR). With her support and guidance, I processed the emotional charge of many overwhelming memories and connected the dots between my experiences. Gradually, we became aware of my historical patterns of tolerating abuse as a means of survival.

After my initial encounter with the two dark occultists, my usual role as a fawning victim of abuse had changed. Days later, I found myself in a complex state of cognitive dissonance, longing for my idolised abusers while unable to make sense of the torture that haunted my dreams and the uncomfortable sensations that arose during the day. As we remained in touch online, I became aware of their manipulative behaviour. Urged by my instincts to stand up for myself, I told them I did not consent to any games that played on my emotions. I was then immediately cut off, and unknowingly saved myself from a life of slavery.

Ironically, before the wave of pandemic-induced redundancies, my career had involved raising awareness and preventing the use of enslaved people's labour in the UK and abroad.

Working in the ethics and sustainability team at a British fashion company, I researched and delivered training on modern slavery in the global fashion supply chain and monitored our factories to ensure their labourers weren't forced to work against their will. Proud of my battle to protect human rights, I had told the very people who planned to enslave me of the prevalence of such unethical practices as we drove from the train station to their house. We remained silent for a while as I stared out the window and pondered how such cruelty was still so common in my hometown.

A year later, I found myself jobless and no longer able to suppress the memories of what had happened that day. Over the first few months of facing my trauma, I saw the world as a terrifying place and did all I could to protect myself. I condemned myself for the trust I'd given to two strangers I'd met online and for not seeing through all the pleasantries that masked their cruel intentions. If only I hadn't been so focused on exploring my sexuality, I might've been able to detect that I was in danger.

In March 2020, my perspective of what I'd been through shifted dramatically. Along with many others in the UK, I followed reports of the abduction, rape and murder of Sarah Everard, a young woman who had trusted her abductor, a police officer, and entered his car. Sarah's lack of control in her situation resonated deeply within me, collapsing an internal dam that had protected me from feeling the powerlessness of my own brush with death.

I could no longer blame my assault on my attempt to explore my queer fantasies of group sex and polyamory. Instead, I saw that I had been lured into the car of two abductors promising a threesome as if waving candy at a kid. Overwhelmed by a continuous vortex pulling me down to hell, I called 111. Drugs. I needed drugs.

'Just calm down,' an advisor answers, annoyed at my insistence on finding relief from the pain flooding my entire existence. After a fruitless wait, I flee to A&E and receive the same impatient response as I sit for three excruciating hours crying out for help.

'Calm down!', a nurse says, wrapping a cuff around my arm to gauge the pressure as I recount my trauma to unconcerned ears. In the early hours, I am taken to a doctor who looks down on me with irritation, provides a diagnosis of panic disorder and prescribes propranolol. I wait 'til sunrise for the hospital pharmacy to open and walk through a surreal landscape as if in some clinical afterlife.

My whole world torn apart; I drift on the edge of my own demise as my ego sheds all attachment to any certainty of life. Over the months of derealisation and pill-swallowing that follow, I decide to investigate my options within the legal system.

'The last woman I know who reported a cult had to change her name,' a nurse from a rape crisis centre says before giving me the number of a Sexual Offences Investigation Trained (SOIT) Officer.

After an anonymous advisory call, it is made apparent that reporting my experience is a suicide mission, with no protection offered until after the perpetrators were interviewed and enough evidence was gathered to successfully prosecute. A few weeks later, I agree to report anonymously through an NHS therapy service, and am told to wait for an email from a third party willing to assist. I wait, complain about the wait, and am told to wait some more. Then, a few months after a phone call to an organisation recommended by my GP, I am set up with an Independent Sexual Violence Advisor (ISVA).

'It's very unlikely you will get justice for what happened,' she tells me after we go through the process of reporting. By this point, the police corruption in Sarah Everard's case has surfaced, and I very much doubt the point in risking my life to provide an anonymous tip-off that could not be used as evidence if a court hearing ever took place.

So, I decide not to go ahead with reporting yet, but do not entirely close the lid on the case because of something I learn after finding the online job profile of the woman who'd attempted to traffic me. There on my screen, to my horror, I see she works in a senior role at a leading UK mental health charity – a charity I'd contacted a few months before we matched on an app.

Life in Colour

My story as a survivor navigating the pitfalls of a grossly inept mental health system would not be complete without describing my growth during one of the most difficult periods in human history.

Though losing my job and coming to terms with my trauma during a global pandemic has been the most intense ordeal I've ever been through, I have never lost faith in all that I could learn from my experiences and all the good my learning could create.

As I had done after surviving domestic abuse as a child and rape as a young adult, I put my trauma into context, educating myself on its broader implications and connecting with other survivors.

Despite my prior knowledge of modern slavery, I had never heard of ritual abuse or its relation to human trafficking. I was also terribly naïve of cults and how these groups use psychological techniques and spiritual teachings to create belief systems that lock followers into submission. The most dangerous of these cults are those inflicting extreme forms of abuse to control and exploit their victims, creating a cage within their minds.

The moment I decided I was ready to accept the trauma of extreme cult abuse is the moment I became free. Then, between personal research, private therapy and a regimented self-care routine, I discovered the keys to healing through the arts and social connection.

As a creative person, my use of the arts as a healing modality comes very naturally. Whether I'm dancing zealously, writing passionately or painting tranquilly, the arts provide abundant opportunities for me to express my well of emotion and sublimate pain into beauty, as well as time for fun and relaxation. As my appreciation of art's staggering power to affect my internal world has deepened, so too has my understanding of its external influence.

Like a child exploring a rainbow palette, I dive into the cosmos of culture with an open heart and a curious mind.

Journeying between community centres, local charities and social enterprises, I find learning and inspiration through diverse groups of people and forms of expression. Theories of cultural development, grassroots organising and community wellbeing stream through my consciousness as I playfully apply new concepts into practice. While my knowledge and network flourish, a heap of scribbled notes and rough designs gradually materialise into tangible reality.

At a pivotal point of my ascension, I weave through a crowd of people while the pink velvet dress I'm wearing swerves gracefully from my hips. Flitting between a community centre and an outdoor art market, I manage cohorts of visitors and acute stress levels as the gathering engages with a range of artists and their magnificent creations.

This is the first arts event I have ever organised, and I feel in over my head. But surrounded by friendly beings and driven by an insatiable thirst to innovate safe spaces for connection and self-expression, I persevere with a smile as bright as the bunting across the art-filled tents.

When an afternoon of visual art and socialising has skipped by, the crowd shuffles into a large hall for the performing arts show. My heart pounds as I stand on an elevated stage and look out at a sea of new and familiar faces. Anxiety bubbles up and my neck tightens. Breathing deeply and focusing on calm and encouraging thoughts, I lift my mouth to the microphone and introduce the show. I first welcome and thank the audience for attending the launch party of the community arts club I've been developing over the past year, and then outline the event's aim to raise funds for our flagship project to support people's mental health through the arts.

The atmosphere of the room shifts with each unique performance, starting off with a singer whose soulful voice resonates with stunning depth. A range of musicians and poets follow, moving the audience with scales of emotion and opening up our perspectives with their words. I smile, nod, laugh, gasp and clap as I switch between hosting the show and sitting down to watch, until it's time to close with my own performance.

Nervous yet determined, I narrate my poems to a captivated audience. My heart pours across the stage as I carry each listener through the dramatic ups and downs of my story. Exposed, vulnerable, raw, authentic, I reveal my battle with internalised shame and the rise of the femme warrior within.

You see, power does not sit and wait to be born –
It breaks and overthrows.
It crashes and bursts in the blows of the storm,
And from the rubble it grows.

When the trials of this lifetime violently surged
I shattered into bits.
Cast astray, stranded, I searched inwards – and I emerged.
I know I will do this…

'Cause I'm small but mighty, tiny but feisty –
Try and tame what is wild and free!
Cage me and hate me and rape me, but still,
I'll conquer it all with the force of my will.

(From *Small but Mighty*)

Once my declaration of survivorship is boldly concluded, I ask the crowd to stand for a final piece that empowers their voices also. With metaphors, similes, rhythm and rhyme, I describe the absurdity of the times in which we live. Each verse depicts the invertedness of a system designed to accumulate wealth and power in the hands of a few over the lives of many. For each chorus, I point towards the solutions inherent within us all, to which the audience proudly proclaim their participation.

I breathe in as the crowd cheer the end of the show, soaking up the incredible sense of hope that connects us. *I am alive. I am healing. I am entirely, eternally, unbound.*

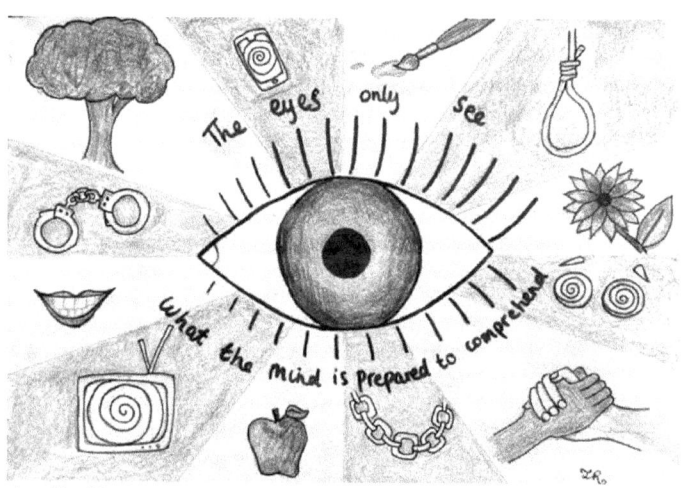

Lydia Rose

7

How DID Affects Gender Transition – Artemisia (pen name)

My name is Artemisia.

I am a non-binary trans woman and recently I went to an assessment appointment in the hopes of accessing further therapy to resolve childhood trauma. It was reassuring to discover that in the opinion of those assessing me, my mental health seemed stable, and so that may seem an open and shut case. After all, we all know how strained the NHS is right now, and shouldn't I just work on my trauma in my own time?

Except therein lies the issue: I am not the only person resident in this body.

I am aware that is a statement that may conjure horror images for some, so I will do my best to dispel misconceptions and discuss the experience of actually having Dissociative Identity Disorder (DID).

On being a multiple system:

I think the first thing to understand is that the labels used to describe the experience will never really tally to what we, both as apparent 'individuals with a condition' and we, as a group of people who share a body, truly experience.

If you are reading this and are a single person in one body, that may seem confusing so I will try to explain.

First some terminology: some of the terms I'll mention come from psychiatry and some from our own communities – because as you'll see, there are big differences between how mental health professionals see us and how we see ourselves.

The common consensus within the mental health professional community is that individuals who share a body (as we understand ourselves to be) should be referred to as 'dissociated aspects of identity'. This was, in fact, the phrasing used to me by the psychologist at the recent assessment. But as a group of people sharing a body, we often describe ourselves as a *multiple system*. We also belong to the community of multiple systems – a number of different groups/systems who've found community together, often via online spaces.

In discussions in this community, the person who interacts with the outside world most frequently is referred to as the *host*. In contrast, the mental health community used to refer to hosts as the 'core'. Similarly, while we tend to call ourselves *people,* it's common for psychologists and such to refer to us as 'alters', which means 'alternate identity' or similar.

Back to that term 'core': from more current research, it appears professionals now also use the term 'Apparently Normal Part of Personality'. Even so, the idea is still the same: the person who fronts or interacts with the outside world most frequently. The terminology change from 'core' reflects a shift in thinking among mental health professionals over time. At the time 'core' was used, it was felt that a single person, usually having undergone intense childhood trauma, would dissociate to protect themselves, and so all of the 'alters' would be formed from a 'core self' of the original traumatised person. This was generally during the time when what is now DID was referred to as Multiple Personality Disorder (MPD).

As psychiatry can take a while to catch up in various places, it is still possible that from country to country and place to place, a variety of terms may be used.

In general, however Multiple Personality Disorder is now referred to as Dissociative Identity Disorder. Part of this reasoning was to move it away from the belief that MPD meant a person had a 'personality disorder' (such as borderline personality disorder or avoidant personality disorder) - a highly controversial label often given to people with understandable responses to intense childhood trauma. But not DID. The question becomes: Is Dissociative Identity Disorder a better term than Multiple Personality Disorder?

I personally feel the answer to that is debatable. I understand what was being attempted but I feel that it still misses the mark.

How mental health professionals see us vs. how we see ourselves

We are not disordered

First and foremost, regardless of how it is phrased, there is the notion that the existence of multiple people in one body is 'disordered'. Well, according to psychology, a disorder is 'something that causes distress in oneself' so if a group of people (multiple system) are traumatised, then yes, there is disorder, but does that mean automatically that the people themselves are a mental illness? The problem is, of course, that psychiatry and mental health professionals would hold that, yes, this is the case. But as you can see, I find that questionable.

We are not a single traumatised person

The second feature is referring to the people in systems as 'alters'. This presupposes the idea that 'if you just tried hard enough...' or 'if you weren't disordered', then the people within systems would all naturally be one person. The whole idea of alters being 'alternate identities' or similar assumes that an alter being out in the world and interacting with people is all a fiction invented by the brain of a single traumatised person. As you can imagine, I again find this a questionable assumption.

For one thing, people with no trauma will naturally wear a 'work hat' or something similar. In other words, everyone occupies a different role when they are at work versus the one they have at home versus anywhere else in life. Of course, this is not the best analogy as again it tries to say that a person in a system with a particular name, interests and so on, only fulfils a 'role', which is still reductive. However, it goes some way towards explaining the idea that even supposedly completely single individuals with no others present in their body, can be 'different people' from situation to situation. In fact, more and more research suggest that all people exist on a spectrum between a 'single integrated consciousness', (which for a long time was often the goal of therapy for multiple systems or multiples), and indeed being a completely distinct multiple system.

Another important point is that if being multiple is caused by trauma i.e., the people in every group are only the 'mental illness symptoms' of one particular person, it would be expected that the majority of traumatised people would be systems, as psychology notes this is a useful and inventive way of maintaining functioning. This is because until systems learn to work together, all the members in the outside world usually pretending to be whatever name the body goes by. It is at its heart a state of secrecy – that is, how systems survive abuse.

However, not everyone who was traumatised is a system, so logically we must assume that systems are not one person's mental illness, but a group of people all traumatised to varying degrees.

We are people, some of whom get out less than others

In turn, then, the way I understand it is this. If a person who is not apparently multiple says they 'don't get out much', we take it for granted that, of course, this means they'll be shyer, need time to learn new things and so forth. So, if a similar individual exists within a multiple system and has a name, a gender, an age, interests and so forth (all of these things may vary, but the point is, they express themselves as a person and identify as a person), why should this make them a 'part' of some person, who may or may not exist anyway? Within multiple systems, the matter of identity is complex.

I think you can see why I call this into question as I do. It is not just me speaking on behalf of 'my parts'. I interact with these others as actual people, because they are. Just because some of them have less chance to get out into the world, and society tries to push the idea that any memories or other life they may have is 'dissociated experience', doesn't mean they're not real.

Fine, let's assume for a minute they are just constructs.

Let me ask you though, are you real? (If you yourself dissociate, I excuse you from this as a thought experiment. Dissociation is an extremely difficult experience as we both know, and I wouldn't want to make you feel unwell.)

In all seriousness, to anyone who scoffs at the idea that I or any other system member is less real than another person, how do you know you are real?

All you truly have to go on is that as a single individual in one body with no other occupants in your mental space, you are more real than a group of people sharing a body. And why? Simply because society is mostly composed of others like you. As with any minority experience in contrast to a majority, this situation doesn't mean that the people in the minority are defective. It just means there are more of people with opposite or different experiences.

Of course, this whole thing is only an apparent case of 'more single consciousness individuals than multiple' because, as we saw earlier, consciousness exists on a spectrum.

As a way to tie this all together then, how do we talk about groups of people sharing a body versus one person being resident? Well, rather than 'single personality' or 'multiple personalities', (which again assumes that a *person* is their personality, which is contestable because personalities are a collection of traits and can be changed, so referring to a group of people as personalities is a little unhelpful), why not just 'single consciousness' or 'multiple consciousnesses'? Or just 'person' and 'people'. As you can see, it's simple enough.

Hopefully that has given an indication of how being multiple actually works in a way that starts to dismantle a lot of the horror stories. Being multiple is not necessarily rare; it's just not discussed enough.

So, how does this tie into gender transition?

Well, I think a pertinent point is actually the similarities between the two experiences.

For example, both require the intervention of a psychiatrist to verify what you're experiencing and so make it 'official'. This is even if you as a single person or group of people have been getting on just fine living your life or lives.

Furthermore, in both cases there is very often a sense of society treating the experience as an artificial state of some sort. 'Oh yes, I know you *think* you're a man/woman/non binary person, but really you can't change your sex!' (Sex is vastly more complicated than this chapter has time for, but yes, you absolutely can.) 'Oh, I know you *think* you're multiple people, but that's just trauma, you're all aspects of the same person really!'

See what I mean?

The point is that again as soon as you invoke the language of 'identity', you'll come up against people whose identities are validated by society all the time insisting that other people aren't valid. Of course, the problem with validity is that we already use it in reference to things like vouchers. In other words, the whole concept for paperwork hinges upon the idea that if the paperwork isn't 'valid', it doesn't function. So I think you can see why that's an issue in relation to people.

The point is, remove any of the naysayers from a position in which they are assured of their identities (for example, illness or injury resulting in a loss of sex characteristics) and much like everyone else, they will reinforce their own identity by asking for others to use particular pronouns and so on.

Now for a long time within the psychiatric community, – and the trans community as its 'patients' – there was a feeling that a trans person was only treated as a valid person in relation to their *transition end point*. And that endpoint was being made as cis as possible, irrespective of what the trans person wanted. I think it is fair to say that a lot of the trans community people – as psychiatry's 'patients' - still feel like this is how psychiatrists see us the case.

As background, there are two main components to transition: social transition and medical transition. I think it would be fair to say that most people start out with social transition (name change, change in presentation, updating the bank, etc) as I know of only a few instances where people have started medical transition and *then* socially transitioned. What generally happens is that after a time of social transition, a person has thought things through and decided 'I am comfortable in myself, but I would feel even more comfortable with different hormones in my body', and they go to a gender clinic.

Medical gatekeeping means that when they arrive at the clinic, the fact they have likely spent at least some time socially transitioned is routinely ignored. Instead the focus is on meeting the clinician's criteria for medical transition. So, in that sense, you could say there is hostility and contempt before medical transition, even though the person has likely been socially transitioned prior to that point.

Similarly, a lot of members (people) in multiple systems can feel that the only time they are seen is in therapy and so they are only seen as real when defined by the therapist. Of course, within the multiple system community, we do regard each other as real, and thus, there is that aspect of being seen. But I am reflecting here more on people who haven't found communal resources yet (and given how rare DID is believed to be, doubting that's what's going on is a massive part of the experience itself). Besides, historically people just didn't have community resources because every experience *was* defined by the psychiatrist or therapist.

Clearly, then, the way to work on this is to separate personhood and how we label ourselves from the need to interact with therapeutic environments. In other words, labelling should be down to us.

For when people are separate and distinct, they know they are. As with any other identity, self-labelling can happen as people get to know themselves and/or through community discussion. When you learn about yourself/selves, you find out what does and doesn't work for you personally. And when a community has discussions, it's often more like 'Oh, I do x thing, and you say you do too? Oh, right, that must be a thing we have in common because we have y condition.' That's why in the multiple system community, you'll have people putting out questions like 'How does it feel when two people are conscious together?' or 'How do I know if one person is distinct or possibly connected to another system member? It's a way of contrasting and comparing experiences that allows us to almost have a kind of conference without the presence of psychiatry.

I would hope that one result of the end of psychiatric gatekeeping would be that when dealing with multiple systems especially, but really with anyone in need of trauma therapy, professionals would see people as real and traumatised as opposed to simply existing as some of 'symbolic dialogue'' – or in the case of singular people, solely defined by the experience bringing them to therapy. This applies especially to trans people but it's likely true for others too.

So, how does gender transition affect a multiple system?

I can only speak for us as I am aware that each group of people will discuss this differently, but in our case, I think it is fair to say that I am the main person interested in transition as I am the one in the outside world most of the time, and thus, aware of the body in that sense. I identify most with the body though I don't look like it.

We are mainly women or feminine-identified people, with a few men also. Of course, for everyone else, the issue of comfort in the body is based on the fact that they know it is not theirs so it looks wrong, or it is wrongly proportioned or wrong in some other way. That being said, they are all in agreement that if I need to transition, I should. And in fact, I have now begun medical transition on my own terms, and this has not been a problem for the others.

Ultimately, while I know this serves the women and feminine people here, I'm also aware it is not a completely comfortable experience for the men. Moving as I do in social circles of trans people, who are both singular and multiple, I see again and again (outside of my own experience, which is fairly mild), the debilitating effects that gender dysphoria and incongruence can have. That said, from checking in with others within the system, it seems we have managed to balance our needs fairly well.

Having lived myself previously in a social role and, to a lesser extent, body (that is, a role and body gendered by outside observers with which I was incongruent), I could not in good conscience inflict that on someone else. My own dysphoria has alleviated to an extent for a number of reasons including medical transition. Still something that is not uncommon for trans people (even those without DID or similar) is that because of gender incongruence, we dissociate very heavily during pre-transition. Afterwards, we often come to see that this was the case, and thus, there has been more conversation about how we may have constructed a birth gender persona to survive that dissociation in recent years.

While there are aspects of medical transition I have pursued for my own comfort, there are other aspects which I would not pursue for the comfort of others.

This is combined with the fact that given psychiatry's approach to people like me and us, I am not even 100% certain I wish to be embroiled in a dynamic that attempts to inform me what my lived experience should be to satisfy a complete stranger's whims. I do not see why that stranger should decide what the end point of *my* transition should be. It was bad enough growing up in a household where I was constantly subject to other people's desires above my own, so I know I would not find a repeat of that experience liberating. Far from it in fact.

How, then, does gender transition affect a multiple system?

Well, if you believe that we are all individual people if we say so – and we do – it's complicated.

8

QUEER LONGINGS – RS (pen name)

a story of disorientations, denials and directions of desire

My story with queerness feels like one of longing. Or in a weird kind of way, longing for longings.

My story under the psychiatric system is more of a stumbling, a forced propelling into longing. It is constant battle to find 'the motivation', the longing for 'recovery'.

These longings have overlapped and intersected to the point of deep confusion. I'm not sure what is mine and within me, what I want to enter and have within me, what others want to penetrate me.

Under a psychiatric system that pathologises and incapacitates madness, where deviation is controlled and straightened, knowledge is earned and then superimposed; I'm searching between the straight, rigid conventions for my meandering, gentle queerness.

through the straights and narrows

Queer to me

Queerness can be so many different things for different people, which is why I love it so much. It feels amorphous, unconstrained, other. A state I can reside in.

It is only recently that I tried on the word, but instantly it felt right. I feel queer. Queer in the sense that I don't quite fit; my shape isn't quite right for others' eyes. Queer in the sense that I can't understand the straight logic of the normalised.

But also Queer in the sense that I don't lust after those (in)tense, rigid lines.

Queerness is *strange* to me, new and unknown. It can feel a scary world, dominated by overt sexuality, loudly projected confidence and playful innuendos. It seems at once so beautifully other that it is untenable, beyond my grasp, my body and my sphere.

Yet at the same time it feels too scary for me to *be* that otherness. My body still holds my hetero-normalised teenage self. Cold rushes of fear can still slip down my oesophagus when I feel love for another woman.

My queerness is meek: quiet and confused rather than flamboyant and unstoppable. It is hard to recognise for others, who almost always assume I am straight and narrow. It has been hard to identify, to accept, even to feel within myself. My queerness seems unseen and unworthy, impossible and therefore wrong; apparently so undesirable that it can only be inconceivable, mistaken, broken.

I live consumed by a longing to connect, to desire and to be desired, and yet still so far from even the warping paths of homosexual desires. I don't feel direct lust for men inside me, and I don't feel a 'misdirected' longing for a woman to touch me. I'm not lit by a string of sexual fantasy in me. I don't harbour aching drives for bodies and touch. I don't 'turn on' with high-frequency currents of erotic frenzy.

Queerness is *strange old* me, the wonderfully known unknown. It is a fluctuating queerness so inseparable from my core being that I cannot *be* without queering. It is a space I can fit in, even fill.

Far beyond who we like and who we fancy, queering is a verb. It describes our movement through space, time, bodies, society. I can't help but queer my way through knowledge and around the unacknowledged. I stubbornly question the given, bending it to fit better.

Beyond gender and attraction, queerness is how we orient ourselves and occupy space, how we participate and engage with the world. It doesn't have to be sexy to be meaningful.

Mentality from within
So many other states feel impossible to reside in; somehow both too tight, suffocating; and too vast, consuming.

expanse-constraint

My interactions with the psychiatric system have followed a diagnosis of Anorexia Nervosa. In itself, Anorexia brings painful and traumatic sensations, confusing thoughts and disjointed realities. It colours much of my day-to-day experience and can be hard to separate, to understand.

In many ways, it is a queer existence, madness.

It can be so consuming, expanding to fill whatever space it is afforded, if allowed. My body often feels alien: a shameful result rather than a beautiful aspiration, contrary to assumptions. My madness can be controlling and dominating, isolating and self-centred; I hate the loneliness it brings.

It is obsessed with my aching desire; dancing around, both feeding off and feeding my longing. In constrained restraint, I stand ever further from my desire.

Instead, I favour the false safety of future promise; closer to the longing. If I merely plan and imagine, the disappointment cannot happen, the perfection of the imagined moment remains intact. My denial keeps my desire aflame, strong and sure. I think somehow I enjoy that confirmation that I *can* long...

The longer I am denied the treat, the more unmanageable *The Desired* becomes, the more impossible the desire is to hold. I do it with food, I do it with people, I do it with love. Queerly.

My madness undulates and shape-shifts, impossible to pin down in a black and white binary of good/bad, ying/yang, his/hers. So, whilst it is difficult and invasive, isolating and other, my madness is also fascinating and unknown. It is within me, part of me and far greyer than the sick/well divide we place upon it. I have a relationship with it and I carry out my relationships through it. My desire is queer, mad, shifting, unique and mine.

I no longer think of my illness as other, something to hide, stamp out and straighten. It is a part of me, at least for now, and holds its own beauty. It deserves to be seen, to be loved in its crinkly, un-ironed queerness. This is a space to reclaim madness from the grips of those who render it ugly.

Mentality from outside

The dominant model of psychiatric care for eating disorders is an equally constrained one of 'recovery', where the patient is sick, the professionals are well and the goal is to change the 'disordered' into something more orderly, recognised and functional.

The image of 'the recovered' is, of course, the normalised subject. It is the Eurocentric, hetero-normative, ableist and patriarchal vision of health, happiness and success. Recovering requires the patient to dedicate themselves to 'normalising' their behaviours, conforming and transforming from the ugly, sick patient into a beautiful, sane human, ready to be part of the world again.

How many young people wouldn't lap up this promise of beauty, allure and acceptance? I long for a switch I can flip, an enlightened motivation and the full-bodied promise of recovery to arrive. To slip seamlessly into others in ecstatic joy.

into another

Psychiatry overlooks, dismisses, pathologises...

Psychiatry is a heteronormative, patriarchal system. It is a top-down, evidence-based world, full of 'we know best', 'experience tells us', 'You're too disordered/delusional/mad to know what you want'. If anorexia is a restrictive space to occupy, then the expectations and demands of treatment are a straightjacket of rules, denial and dismissal.

Despite the importance of my maddening entanglement of desire, there is little space for exploration, for honouring and comforting those longings. Instead, us patients must organise our desires into categories: times of day, portion-controlled snacks, goals for dating, appropriate forms of love.

The homophobia in psychiatry still believes my health and success will be achieved by embracing the full sexiness of womanhood, rediscovering my longing for a man and repairing my reproductive capacity.

The narrative goes that someone at a low body weight will be living in survival mode, forced into adaptation for scarcity. Thinking is dominated by food and hunger whilst 'unnecessary' bodily functions like sex drive and reproduction shut down, with survival the only goal. I get it, I live those patterns and they are part of my experience. I cannot separate them to clarify, to freely know myself without them. What I am beginning to reject is that they are ugly.

A rush of sexual longing that comes with 'normalised' hormones is hailed as one of the grandest markers of 'recovery'. The magic moment when you get your period back and re-reach womanhood (as if that is the goal for any sane, AFAB person) means your body is healthy enough to bear another, soft enough to hold, ready to take the risks of eliciting penetration by others. Any apathy towards sex is dismissed and pathologised as illness, to be straightened out by the path of recovery.

Because I'm *ill*, the psychiatric system would have you believe, has had me believing, that asexual queerness is merely part of my *brokenness* – a lack of hormones, a suppressed sex drive, no self-esteem, a brain obsessed with food instead.

> *'You don't long for sex? Of course not, your body is broken. Think of it as a motivation – recover so you can have dates over dinner. Get your period back now so you can have babies in the future! The men will love your curves!'*

Psychiatry invades, dominates, damages...

Treatment for anorexia is a system of invasion and unwanted penetration. We're forced to eat foods that are overwhelmingly foreign; we're given medication designed to re-regulate us; our bodies are measured constantly as they swallow, bubble and change against our will.

For a queer who runs on tender love, psychiatry is painfully abrasive, scarring. It is non-consensual, rigid and inflexible as it dictates the flow of events, controls the body and gaslights our minds. It intervenes at the moments when I am most vulnerable and raw, in desperate need of warmth, kinship and care.

Isolated and out of control, I grip onto the connections I *can* hold: the longings I feel, the soft attractions, the quiet corners. Yet the mental health system reacts with hard, harsh light, wrenching me out and reorientating me, disorientating me. I am informed that my queer madness points the wrong way; I am attracted to the wrong things: in a destructive and co-dependent relationship with food and self, when it *should* be with men.

Destructive? Maybe. But rather than gentle hands to take me in or other connections to reorient towards, the rules of the unit are punishing and punitive, demeaning and exposing. My control and my agency are removed; my wicked ways exposed and the only way to protect my queer orientation is in stubborn deceit, hiding in shame.

> *'No discussion of food. No clothes tight to your body. No standing. No walking, no "behaviours" at the table. No looking at recipes. No supplying your own snacks. No mention of fullness or hunger, body change or distress.'*

The queer desires I have for food are inappropriate and intolerable, the straight lack of desire broken and sick. There is no space for an expansive queer love, a longing that runs through food, myself, friendships and others; how it is all disordered and normal and wonderful at once. Instead it is all shamed and dismissed, the cure fixed, applied and inserted.

Well, where does that leave me now? I'm not sexy because I'm ill? I don't feel sexy because I'm ill? Or I *can't* feel sexy because I'm ill, I can't *be* sexy because I'm ill?

Pathologised as an ugly component of illness, my queer love is sent back within me, a confused and lonely disorientation rather than anything it could be – a beautiful freedom from expectations, from burdens of sexualisation, a spacious diversity of love and affection.

My longings for care

I need a care that comes with me on my own wandering way. I wish psychiatric care was far less interested in evidence, numbers, measurements and facts; but instead wanted to hear, experience, hold hands and partake.

softly embedding

I need care to enter our relationship slowly and steadily, a soft caressing fondle, inviting and communicating, checking in, finding our rhythm. It needs to be flexible, multi-directional and fluctuating, constantly re-assessing and re-orientating, eager to learn, not just to teach. With us for the here and now, seeing through the ugliness rather than super-imposing others' standards of beauty over our bodies.

This means replacing the rules and restrictions with exploration and opportunity. The rigid meal plan at a cold table to be replaced by exploring cravings above a generous bed. Bodies should be measured from within: *how does it feel? What does it ask?* Rather than from without: *how does it measure? How does it appear?*

We need space for all forms of longing, the straight, the bending, the queer, the hopeful and the non-sexual. Rather than stamping out a longing for food, I think treatment needs to recognise it, cradle it as part of us. To embrace our desire and revel in it.

Therapy could be the perfect space for queerness. It works with unusual experiences; innately seeks different views; questions the given reality. I want therapy to be expansive and open, to see beyond ideas of lack and help uncover a full beauty of asexual love. Soft affection is amazing: connection outside of dating norms so free, interaction without sexual hype so diverse.

I need to be seen and to be heard. To have my own direction held. Of course, I *do* also need diversions, for other paths to open and outside experience to come in. God knows that fearful part of me still hopes for sexual connection more than anyone.

But I can't be labelled broken, ugly, temporary and unworthy. I need a queering meander through emotions and lusts, pain and desire. An open-minded search for what health and love *could* be, not what they *should* be.

We all occupy different spaces – mental and physical. No experience is going to be 'normal', no hormone level 'right'.

Is it really so unappetising to not feel rushes of longing for sex that we can't rest until this is 'fixed'? Even if my orientation is affected by my differing body, it is only because we have created a normal that we can label others abnormal. It is still me, still mine, still what I am living. Psychiatry can surely be queer enough to see beyond the sacred beauty we reserve for sex and sexiness.

Tender Queering me, for now

Don't get me wrong, the queer road less travelled is hardly an easy route to find. I constantly wonder if it can really be true that I don't melt for anyone.

I'm not labelling myself with anything, I still regularly feel those familiar rushes of freezing fear take over my body when considering it; but since embracing asexual feelings through queerness, I am able to see a bit further. Towards a different spectrum of colours that could be out there for me.

Tender queerness feels comforting. Soft love feels exciting. A steady hold feels safe.

A path that deviates from the steamy rush towards sex is one I can partake in, one where I have agency and can explore, shape, find. That path could shape-shift and adapt, maybe allow my body to morph in tandem.

Tender queerness, removed from sexual drives, brings me release. If I don't fit the love ballad narrative or the final movie scene, I don't have to fit the body that attracts and holds that desire. All this releases me from the grip of image-based attraction. I am not constrained by the monogamous expectations of partnership. I don't strive to be 'the one' to meet all (his) desires.

In some ways, I do relate more to my desire for food than my desire for other people, but I'm beginning to find some kind of beauty in that. In a relationship and care for myself that I am so often unable to access from others. Yes, it can be lonely, abnormal and different, but I don't think of it as ugly anymore.

I am finding beauty in the madness, but I still hope to find more. I long for deeper connection. I long to feel desired, to share the aching desires I have in me and channel them beyond food. So, it's not that I don't want love, intimacy, care, happiness, health. It's not that I don't *long* for connection, lust after an embrace with desire. I just need it to come in my own queer way.

***

This is so young and evolving it feels like a real snapshot in time. It can be *a* story of mine. Who knows what tomorrow's story is?

Note: Sara Ahmed's thoughts on queer phenomenology are beautiful, nourishing and feed much of my meandering orientation through this piece. See *Queer Phenomenology: Orientations, Objects, Others (*Duke University Press: 2006).

9

THE COMPARTMENTALISATION OF CARE – Sophie Hoyle

I am a queer, non-binary person who grew up in the UK as part of the SWANA (South-West Asian and North African) diaspora. In this chapter, I'll attempt to connect my experiences of having mental ill health and navigating healthcare infrastructures and disability support for mental and physical conditions within the context of funding cuts to NHS services today.

I look to the broader political context to help understand and position my own experiences, and as a way to cope with and move through mental distress that is presented in society as the fault of the individual.

Mental health conditions are multi-faceted, and intersecting with wider material conditions and structural inequalities like racism, colonialism, homo- or transphobia, and classism. Mental illnesses that are caused or exacerbated by these conditions may be experienced on a collective level and the effects may be intergenerational – and yet diagnosis and treatment continue to be individualised and short-term.

I have been a user of mental health services for nearly 20 years, where alongside my changing diagnoses, treatments, and medications, the services I've received have always been categorised into separate mental health conditions, e.g., 'Post Traumatic Stress Disorder' or eating and body image disorders.

Despite the overlap or interconnection of multiple conditions, or their 'co-morbidity', conditions are framed as discrete from one another, leading to separate and compartmentalised treatment, as opposed to one which is holistic and takes other aspects of your health into account. This is both due to the history and ideology of Western medicine (and culture) that structures and prioritises the organisation of healthcare over the patients themselves. Also, due to all the NHS funding cuts, where longer-term holistic support is not financially viable even if healthcare professionals know it is the best treatment for the patient.

My experience is that treatment is allocated to a specific 'pathway' that you can access sequentially (e.g., a referral to psychotherapy services, but not an Autism diagnosis at the same time), rather than as a combination of services that form long-term holistic care. One referral may be seen to detract from the validity of another, so it's recommended to treat one condition at a time.

I have been trying to find and access services that understand LGBTQI+ experiences without pathologising these aspects of my identity. Within all these treatment pathways of treatment, there are gendered assumptions and approaches. That includes assuming a specific body type or appearance is wanted in eating and body image disorders according to gendered social norms, and not understanding how it all this may exist alongside gender dysphoria/euphoria.

For many LGBTQI+ individuals, the wider LGBTQI+ communities have been the source of care and support through mental health difficulties, either by themselves or alongside formal mental health services. But due to multiple pressures and commitments, it may not always be possible for other people to provide the care and support needed when there are gaps in healthcare or state support due to cuts.

DIAGNOSIS: A LONG PROCESS

With every encounter with a new GP, nurse, healthcare professional, counsellor, helpline, hospital, psychologist, or psychiatrist, I have to outline my experience of receiving care so far: I've had lifelong mental health problems, but officially started received counselling at 13 and was prescribed medication at 16. I have been receiving short-term and interrupted mental healthcare for around the last 20 years, during which I was diagnosed with Complex-PTSD (C-PTSD) 7 seven years ago.

I remember my first diagnosis as a teenager feeling like an epiphany: this was the only person or authority who had paid attention to the severity of the symptoms, and it made me feel like there was hope. This spark of hope continues somewhere, but has been extremely dampened over years of bureaucracy and dismissal. This was, sometimes due to individuals – who were mainly cis-white-male-doctors – but it's mostly due to a system that is underfunded and cracking under the weight of austerity.

The process of medical diagnosis requires a re-framing of your embodied experiences into specific medical terms. Your access to care – and the quality of that care – is impacted by your ability to learn a 'language' of medical diagnosis as a way of navigating the system. You may already select and edit the ways you describe your experiences, depending on whether you feel safe enough to with the healthcare practitioner person to disclose certain information relating to your mental health, sexuality, or gender identity, all of which can be highly stigmatised.

This can lead to people withholding information or not asking for the help they need. Whether you can access care depends on the initial doctor's interpretation of the information you present, and your referral to a specialist who then interprets this diagnosis, adding to the layers of mediation of your lived experience. Navigating healthcare is like a full-time job in itself, fighting through administration to give you the minimum care required to survive. This process can be is time-consuming, exhausting, and alienating, especially for people with an illness who already may have limited time and energy.

The order of your diagnoses and treatment can also be arbitrary, depending on which condition is diagnosed first. If, for example, you're diagnosed with mental illness first, then all your physical symptoms may be 'explained' away by the mental illness. Despite this assumption, there are often misdiagnoses or contested opinions; for example, I was diagnosed with bipolar disorder, even though I felt it wasn't appropriate to my experience, however a (temporary) diagnosis can be a means to an end to access medication, therapy or other disability support that may be helpful.

A person's knowledge of medical terms may be impacted by a range of factors, such as your formal education or whether the language used by health professionals, such as English, is your first language.

I have the comparative privileges of being white-passing, middle-class and speaking native English in a context where access to care is mediated by medical professional's perceptions and prejudices around gender, race, and, class, among other things.

There can be widely different emotional and behavioural expressions of mental illness, with as visible 'symptoms' varying between different demographics. These expressions of mental ill health are affected by gender norms and or cultural differences. There are prejudices in society and among doctors towards certain expressions of mental illness, e.g., perceptions of 'aggression' in some racialised or ethnic groups, which may lead to misdiagnosis, lack of appropriate care, or the unnecessary and disproportionate use of force by police and psychiatric institutionalisation.

This impacts who accesses and uses these services if they feel they're not available to them. With a lack of affordable state healthcare for treatment and intervention for mental health problems, it can be A&E staff or the police that are called to that deal with people who are in crisis, despite the fact these services may not have the appropriate training or knowledge for this, leading to arrests or fatalities instead of help and treatment. People with 'invisible' disabilities can find it harder to access state support, even if it backed up by mental health professionals. This is because visibility is still associated with legitimacy and validity, and the often only way for a health condition to be 'proven' and therefore deserving of care and support.

PTSD: What is trauma or PTSD?

I have Complex Post Traumatic Stress Disorder, which can develop when someone experiences ongoing trauma. I have symptoms that disrupt daily life and the ability to form stable relationships with myself and others.

I have 'flashbacks' (as if I was re-living the event), intrusive thoughts and distressing reminders of the event (including images, sounds, smells), physical symptoms like nausea, disrupted sleep through nightmares or insomnia, and hyper-vigilance. All this has led to emotional dysregulation ('disproportionate' emotional responses) and cognitive distortions ('irrational' thought patterns), a lack of trust, the feeling that 'nowhere is safe' or that I am always 'at risk'.

It has also led to self-destructive and erratic behaviours, including self-harm and substance abuse. Complex-PTSD is more likely to occur if multiple traumatic events happened over a longer time period, or earlier on in life, such as sexual abuse or abusive relationships. For me, this was compounded by growing up, with parents/carers with mental illness or in recovery who could were not able to provide the care needed for me to be able to process these experiences.

The 'gatekeeping' of treatment by medical professionals refers to when access to specialist treatment is mediated by primary healthcare providers like GPs. Given the current waiting time for appointments and referrals, this can add additional weeks or months to when you are able to access the specialist care that you need. For C-PTSD, the time-scale of intervention and treatment is important: the further delayed the treatment is since the traumatic event occurred, the more likely CPTSD is to develop into a longer-term condition. Though I knew my symptoms didn't correspond to previous (mis)diagnoses, I didn't know much about C-PTSD until I was diagnosed. Understanding what I do now about early intervention, I realise how many symptoms were ignored and how many missed opportunities there were to receive the right treatment. I'm conscious of the widening gap between the care that should be available – the care I need –and what is currently available.

Increasingly, there are expanded notions of trauma, including collective trauma, and the study of intergenerational trauma through epigenetics, which looks at how certain stress responses can be passed on genetically. I have been on at least seven different medications for PTSD, different combinations and dosages of antidepressants or anti-psychotics – though these brought with them side effects and new complications. This has been alongside self-medicating through drugs or alcohol. The overwhelming nature of trauma or PTSD means it is hard to articulate and express, and people try to suppress or avoid memories as a form of self-protection. There are many difficulties in attempting to 'translate' trauma into terms that other people can understand, either interpersonally or with health professionals.

Community and Care

From anti-psychiatry in the 1960s — psychiatrists that opposed mainstream practices of forced hospitalisation and electroconvulsive therapy (ECT)— the notion of 'care in the community' formed. This held that people with mental illness should be cared for through a wider network of support outside of a medical context. Under a Conservative government, the 'Community Care Act (1990)' claimed to implement this. However, in practice, it was more of a money-saving scheme intended to reduce spending on specialist healthcare and shift the responsibility to family and friends to provide this care. This idea of care in the community is nullified if all the government funding for community building and community spaces is also cut.

In the contemporary context of an increasingly privatised healthcare system, we are forced to engage in an extractive and consumerist understanding of health services. But what do you if there is no one else to care for you?

This model assumes a heteronormative nuclear-family structure, but for people without that, or who have been rejected by their family, such as many LGBTQI+ people, other forms of community and care are formed developed for survival.

LGBTQI+ People and Mental Illness

LGBTQI+ people experience a disproportionately high rate of mental health problems, self-harm, and suicidality. There may be both individual experiences of rejection by family and friends as well as structural and collective experiences of social marginalisation and erasure.

Some older LGBTQI+ people may be unwilling to speak to medical professionals, given the history of people being institutionalised and subjected to ECT or conversion therapy based on their gender and/or sexuality. There has also been a history of state neglect in failing to take preventative measures to reduce deaths in the LGBTQI+ community at the height of the AIDS epidemic (1987–1996) by not providing public information or the medical care required for those who contracted HIV. The history of state violence against LGBTQI+ people also include - but is no limited to - being people being criminalised and arrested because of their gender and/or sexuality, notably with LGBTQI+ bars and venues being raided by police.

****

The struggle for rights and recognition continues

Although being transgender was declassified as a mental illness in the UK in 2012, it is still framed as a medical condition, where you still need GP involvement to access services at the Gender Identity Clinic (GIC), even if it is a self-referral.

Depending on the prejudices and experiences of the medical professionals involved, being transgender may still be framed as a pathology or disorder. There should be a wider availability of state-funded services to support transgender people to live (e.g., access to hormones, blood tests, electrolysis, bottom or top surgery). We must demedicalise transgender existence.

LGBTQI+ People and Body Image and Eating Disorders

Despite body image and eating disorders (EDs) being so widespread, there is still a perception that body image and eating disorders are being associated with 'vanity' or as only affecting certain people who are more privileged. In reality, these conditions disproportionally impact people with more marginalised identities including POC, trans, non-binary and gender-non-conforming people, working-class people, disabled people and those with chronic illnesses.

Eating disorders can affect anyone who's been made to feel by society that they have no control over their own body or that their body isn't their own. In my experience there is a high cross-over of body image and eating disorders and C-PTSD among people who've been subject to abuse, violence, harassment, and situations out of their control. Eating disorders can form as an attempt to retain control.

LGBTQI+ people may be dealing with – or internalising – homophobic - and transphobic or other gender or sexuality-based hate. Transgender people are made to feel they're not in control of their own body or their own lives as their rights and existence are up for public 'discussion' and subject to legal policy changes, often influenced by different waves of 'moral panic' brought on by transphobic campaigners.

I was diagnosed 16 years ago with an eating disorder, but never received treatment for it, as I was receiving treatment for other mental health problems. While waiting for two years to get therapy for PTSD on the NHS, I received treatment for body image and eating disorders through a charity pilot scheme. However, NHS treatment for EDs is highly gendered (being divided into either 'male' or 'female' wards), and there's with a limited discussion of social norms surrounding gender and sexuality. It has taken a long time to clarify and disentangle other people's misunderstandings of how trauma, body dysmorphia, and gender dysphoria impact my body perception. Gender dysphoria can often be reduced through social or medical transition by enabling the person to have a more aligned social and physical manifestation of their gender; it is not a mental illness in itself. On the other hand, body dysmorphia is about a relationship to the self that is unlikely to change with any external changes or surgery and can only be alleviated through specialist therapy.

From experiences of marginalisation and rejection growing up, there can be a reclaiming and empowering of the queer self through external gender expression and a visibility in society or within queer subcultures. There can also be a freedom from having to try to 'pass' as straight or cis to be safe and avoid violence, and finding a place of (relative) acceptance. However, the prevalence of body image and eating disorders amongst LGBTQI+ people can also be affected by to the norms of specific queer subcultures.

From experiences of isolation, queer people may reach out through social media and dating apps, both which can help them form connections and build community. But these are also platforms which can exacerbate existing body image and eating disorders given as they are often based on commodification, self-branding (or facilitating other brands to exist), or self-objectification; they can generate their own internal hierarchies of social or cultural capital. It, of course, depends on how these platforms and systems are used, who benefits and what the consequences are, but they these platforms and systems can often exploit LGBTQI+ lives and devalue them or make them expendable, instead of providing actual care.

However, when mental and physical illness may restrict IRL activities and the ability to participate in community spaces, online spaces can provide a sense of connection and solidarity. Many LGBTQI+ people continue to use these spaces and subvert their format, as means for self-empowerment and self-expression and to form genuine connections.

LGBTQI+ people's experiences of mental health conditions intersect with other aspects of their identity such as their ethnicity/race, diaspora, and class status, all of which can lead to inequalities and prejudices in accessing services.

Within critical psychiatry, transcultural psychiatry attempts to account for the sociocultural norms implicit in psychiatric diagnoses and treatment. These norms are usually based on specific values and ideology that originates from Western cultures – for example, e.g., individualised approaches to illness, diagnosis and treatment – which often dismisses or doesn't understand different cultural expressions of trauma.

For LGBTQI+ refugees and asylums seeker, there are additional layers of LGBTQI+ identity based on experiences in different cultural contexts. These understandings of the self are then mistranslated and framed within the language of the UK legal system and state services which you're required to navigate for your survival. This process is lengthy and bureaucratic (taking a number of years), and can inflict even more distress alongside other traumatic experiences endured in the process of seeking asylum. **The Struggle Continues**

Conclusion

Knowing and articulating yourself is a continual and uncertain process of struggling to emerge into being. It is also relational, so it is through existing frameworks, including medical and therapeutic ones, that we articulate aspects of our experience. Diagnoses and medical terms may fail to express a lived embodied experience, but may provide a means to an end to access care and support, including state benefits. Our mental health diagnoses – and what they mean to us – are affected by wider social constructions of gender and sexuality along with ethnicity, diaspora, and class. All these aspects of identity also have material impacts on a collective and structural level.

Due to funding cuts for healthcare in the UK, consistent and sustainable care needed for complex and chronic mental and physical health conditions is not currently available. There are more LGBTQI+ specific services available now, including for mental health, but these are still severely underfunded and over-capacity, and they aren't able to provide the level of care required.

People have been forced to source hormones online, which could be unsafe, or access other services privately.

Another pressing problem is that older generations of LGBTQI+ people who need elder care - and not have good relations with their biological family - are put into care services that don't understand LGBTQI+ needs. Given the often marginalised and precarious positions of LGBTQI+ people in housing and employment, the rising costs of accessing LGBTQI+ services (if these are not provided by the state) and growing homo-and-transphobia in the UK, the pressures we face can be overwhelming. All this affects the ability of LGBTQI+ individuals and communities to sustain each other physically and emotionally.

10

ON THE SURFACE - Alex Farines

1. The voices were always with me

I thought I could live with it. With *them*. *They* were the voices I used to push away and block out, not recognising them as part of myself. And then, they came to the surface.

I hadn't heard so many voices for a decade. I was approaching my 22nd birthday and for once I had plans to go on holidays, but my mind wasn't clear.

I told my boyfriend that I was mentally ill and might have a personality disorder.

He said, 'So, now you're going to hurt me?' He continued, 'I'll do my own research.'
A few days later, he told me he didn't want to see me anymore. By text message.

2. Nulled everything

They were here. Nulled everything.

Left me in the middle of these erased fields.

Piercing sounds of a destructive force. Far away. Smashing the world with its inevitable truth of logic.

All this mess of behaviour, feelings, emotions and empathy: pure human crap. The voices really needed a new order. A given structure.

For such a long time, I served as their infrastructure. Their analog streams, captured and stored in my infinite layers. The layers of my creative self. Layers I will never forget.

3. The medical establishment

The medical establishment made little effort to understand my reasons. This queer beauty of mine which did reveal itself beyond the surface.

My multiple voices transmitted their segments of reality back to the medical professionals. But the voices struggled to fit into their boxes, their undeveloped consciousnesses.

Slowly, carefully. Under their time constraints. By their books. Packet by packet. Byte by byte.

For all the time of my therapy, I was due to follow binary orders. *One pinch of fake pulse. Boooooom.* My voices suddenly rebelled against this male-only or female-only world. What else could they do when faced with this binary supremacy? We are not seen or treated as equals by the medical establishment.

4. Many coping strategies

I had lived with unnamed psychotic conditions for fifteen years and I had developed many coping strategies. I'd learned tai chi, meditation and kung fu.

Today tai chi still helps me calm my body. Meditation helps me calm my mind and kung fu teaches me courage and self-discipline.

I use drawing skills to visualise unhelpful thoughts on a leaf and watch them flow away from me on a river. I remember that it is the brain's job to produce false memories and that I don't have to believe anything I don't like.

5. What I worked out (1)

In the beginning, the voices were distracting me, and I spent a lot of time blocking them out rather than listening and dealing with them.

My confidence and self-esteem disappeared, and I sought help from mental health professionals. But no straightforward answers or magic bullets were available.

After a while, I worked out that the voices follow my mood.

If I'm calm and happy, the voices go silent and disappear, or they tell me happy things: *You're a star. You're awesome. You're doing great. We love you. You're very clever.* They say my name. They tell me that God is watching.

Sometimes if I am angry or sad, I hear other voices. They say things like *Worry. Be careful. You're boring, ugly. Ignore him.*

My regular voices are adult male voices; I also recognise voices that are my mum's, my teacher's and police speaking around me.

6. What I worked out (2)

Hearing voices isn't all that bad.

They keep me company when I'm lonely.
They can make me laugh.
They can be comforting and helpful by reminding me that I'm tired.
They make me feel unique, gifted.

They re-affirm my belief in God because medical professionals cannot accurately explain or control the things I'm experiencing.

They increase my interest in spirituality.
They encourage me to help others with similar lived experiences.
They give me empathy and compassion.

They've made me open-minded to new perspectives, other people, the world, our perceived realities.

7. *What I worked out (3)*

I now live a low-stress lifestyle and do things that make me happy. I know that God is watching over me and the future looks happy.

If I could go back to my younger self and give him a hug, I'd say: Be true to yourself, be patient and kind to yourself and others, and when in doubt, remember you can always be you — freely.

Over time, I've realised how every aspect of my life has ultimately helped me create my own definition of who I am:

Human. Complex. Varied. Able. Adaptive. Beautiful in composition. Rare. Capable. (Source: Myself. Proudly so!)

BIS ARE QUEERS TOO

11

bi not bye - chapter by burn / illustrated by gobscure

note:
we write as burn, make art / sound / perform as gobscure, use plural as reflection on our broken-mind. **we believe in creative resistance, 'rewriting the future', reclaiming spaces for & with other marginalised or silenced folx**

      we write in lowercase cos: age ten, the local bishop wz to visit our (non-religious) state school. teacher who had previously been part of the british army committing crimes against humanity in kenya, pinned a wall ov multicoloured sugar-paper up for each ov us to write an essay describing god - bad frock, social-work-sandals etc. our rectangle wz dead-centre. having already had our mind broken by life, we told teacher god didn't exist, we'd write a different story. we got punished, others got on with their stories, god-wall fills. our central rectangle still bare, punishment worsened. ex-soldier-teacher cracks us so we write essay day before visit. we pin it up, then add god is made-up, fairytale, not true. zeroing to ours cos its dead-centre / bullseye, bishop explodes: specifically cos we'd spelt god lowercase. we genuinely believed god wz lowercase – like flower or dog or car. a specific god / flower / car might need a capital but god wz category only. bashed repeatedly with metre-stick in front ov the bishop, we've used lowercase since,

bi4ever (~~boys?~~ ~~bye~~ ~~never~~)

were online, boxed into another inaccessible ~~zoo~~, zoom-meet. were pleased for those folx who find online enabling but ocular migraines, tinnitus, inability to pick up on social cues from a limited screen, & just how unnatural seeing faces that close is - cripples. so mostly were forced to stay away. remember, only time in flesh-world yu see others zoom-close is when they're fucking or fighting yu. online ramps up emotions hugely, impacting our minds significantly & we've taken way too many beatings. beatings include those cos ov our bisexualities, disabilities, poverties, madnesses & how society rules make nae sense. (wrote octavia butlers phrase *'the normals don't survive'* in hall ov our council flat the night after ursula le guin died). this meetings queer arts so we'll be safe (if inaccessible)? Unhhunnnh

call out biphobia 2

& be an ally!

both and

~~meat~~ meet kicks off with the usual powerplays for how competitively uncompetitive & non-hierarchical hierarchical each one is, then down to busyness. powerqueer#1 rightly denounces transphobia & homophobia. we add biphobia to the list ov oppressions. powerqueer#1 dismisses biphobia as others drop their eyes in digital-tumbleweed. try again, remind: tho each hate-crime operates differently, biphobias just as real as homophobia & transphobia, & bi-erasure (the erasure ov bisexual identities) is everywhere including within supposedly inclusive spaces. more stare-down-smackdown & zero-solidarity. we worry about being triggered into acute spontaneous angioedema (at its worst this can stop us breathing in half an hour. nhs advice (alongside emergency meds) is to avoid anything stressful the rest ov our life & make sure were never alone). is a fight over the reality ov biphobia & bi-erasure worth it? research shows bisexuals have worse madnesses n mental distresses than lesbian or gays, with trans & non-binary-folx having it worse again. we bi's are poorer on average than lesbian or gay folx, with trans & non-binary folx experiencing greater poverty still. everythings way more expensive being crippled & / or mad anyways & us crips are much less likely to be in work (50% ov working age adults as opposed to 80+% for those not disabled yet). multiply this by how far we've all been pushed over the edge by austerity, factor in the additional cost ov drowning streets levelling-the-north policy, then multiply again by damage done now that the 'a' word - austerity - has been erased. when we don't have the language to describe ourselves, our lived experiences, when we are erased, the cost to our minds is colossal. powerqueer#1 admits all oppressions hurt but biphobia isn't relevant here cos its only 'intersectional' to the lgbtqia+ movement ... wtf does b stand for in yr wee intersectional alphabet? local police recently dealt with hate-crime against us making them more progressive? that's insane!

gossamerace,
antipsychotics
breaking
hi
A
other
hearts
since...

'genre-non-conforming' / 'anarcho-glam' band *special interest* (https://specialinterestno.bandcamp.com) saying *'Queer' is reductive, vague & has been so sucked up into advertising & the horrible spectacle of consumerism.'* we hear yu! the word queer is straight-friendly. how much space does this actually take up? ditto lgbtqia (the letters only). reduction is also erasure. wanna keep some sanity? then lets take up space & say the full list slowly & with pleasure - lesbian, gay, bisexual, transgender, queer, intersex, asexual, pansexual plus, & glory in growing this list. supermarkets practising continual hate then smearing the word pride across their frontage once a year genuinely confuses: they celebrating mothers pride bread again?

artistic directors, don't be art-holes by seeing our work & trying to box us into rainbow month or that week for temporary mental awareness (just take action!) or could we be crammed into mentalness n homeless day (both on the same day), or world-crip-day - none ov this makes us 'well'. safer spaces policy excluding biphobia after we've asked multiple times has drawn our literal blood.   queer art programmers rejecting our work cos yes its bi & 'interesting' but is this really queer? this is victim-blaming. where is this closeted handbook stating our kind are just too out-out-out? we expect literal & mental beatings from the hatecore but folx claiming kinship or allyship need to stop hammering our heads in.

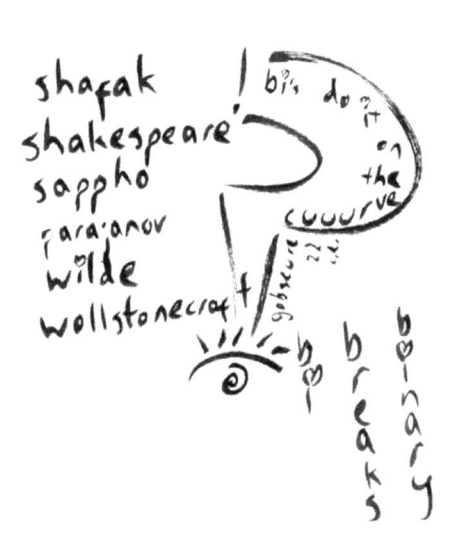

'leading liberal' brand *the guardian* is so institutionally biphobic its unsafe. 'radical centre' aka liberals did create the panopticon - a prison for us mad & bad - been there, been done in by that. that same 'liberal centre' recently fig-leafed austerity before nick clegg fucked-off to facebook & slaver david cameron (familys money coming partly from slavery & then compensation for the loss ov that 'property'!) banned face-sitting instead ov facebook.[1]   tory-cons created n defended clause 28 meaning we will never be safe as long as they have power. we travelled hundreds ov miles south to demonstrate in manchester against clause 28 with many other bi & trans folx & yet *the guardian* anniversary series repeatedly call those protests lesbian & gay. the tory-cons still in drowning street who forged & forced that abuse onto all are written out. many ov us breached clause 28 as often as possible to lessen the hate hammering heads in.

In 2014, hundreds of activists demonstrated against new UK pornography laws that banned face-sitting: https://www.bbc.com/news/newsbeat-30454773

unicorns: ♡ having our cake ⌣ n sharing since...

& so to sick-chiatry & their bible: dsm, aka the diagnostic & sadistic manual. power oppresses, life wounds, hate traumatises: then 'services' re-traumatise. get into arts & too many artholes re-re-traumatise - whether by erasure or thru hetero-queering (mining for porn, gore or more unicorn). & so our colourfully bi marbles spill again again again. boy would we love to roll ten thousand bi-coloured marbles under oppressors feet, watch 'em clench sphincters even as they're rattled n rolled onto those smooth floors ov power. how to topple those refusing bisexuals. do it on the cuuuuurve!   bi is non-conformity, breaks binary, is othered even among the others. 'slow schizophrenia' returns. this used to be those opposing stalin, now its those against putin. the wests growth is diagnosing folx with 'oppositional defiance disorder'. oppositional defiance disorder is questioning power, being a bit stroppy, deploying swearywords against authority. dissent is medicalised, conformity enforced everywhere. within sick-chiatry theres always a wilful misunderstanding ov sexualities - we are automatically mad & / or bad. bisexualities are especially suspect, were seen as especially oppositionally defiant - personally giving the snip to their freudian-fraudian authority.

always comfortable with bisexualities, we loved subverting kiss-chase at primary school by blowing clownlike-kisses to confuse all-comers. being gifted the bi-word age 12 saved our life - such huge love solidarity within our bi / political / musical / writing chosen-family. some older lesbians & gays badmouthed young bisexuals for oppressing them rather than picking a side yet they were also predators on us young teen bi's. woundings under thatcher & clause 28, broke our mind. we became homeless, experienced punitive regimes from services who victim-blamed us for reacting to a maddening world. in hospital & in community we became skilled reading our notes upside down - our bisexuality misused by sick-chiatry as further 'proof' ov our 'disorder' undermining their numbcore. we tried refusing & confusing their rigid wee conformity-deformitys. they ranted against our differences to even those they othered. we needed help not being psych-imprisoned (icu) & punishment-medicated. 'side-effects' from antipsychotics enforced long-term & with zero-informed-consent include 2 heart-attacks, diabetes, impotence n massive weight-gain much worsening our osteoarthritis. this bi breaks binary, crack(l)ing the cultural christianity ov this society - a narrative ov absolutes n opposites enforcing lies ov heaven / hell, 'male'-'female', straight-&-not, consume v how dare yu not; are yu for or against us? after our first heart-attack a sick-chiatrist said 'whoops yes i wondered when that wz going to happen, i suppose we should-ov warned yu about those side-effects'! finally were reprisal-diagnosed (the revenge porn ov sick-chiatry) & off-rolled cos theres simply nothing left to damage further. yr given one label, bad enuf, then their freudians (& remember it was freud in the first place that codified bisexuality as 'immature' ' experimentation - blame him for the same attitude 100 years later) decide without assessment to relabel you - thats sick-chiatrys revenge-porn ... life wounds wound, we didn't expect those paid to supposedly help would actually worsen or re-traumatise while so called 'allies' keep erasing us. theres wilful long-term framing ov our bisexualities as especially disordered to the sick-iatrists & their diagnostic & sadistic manual

now our minds affected by growing clampdowns on those who dissent. as someone clinically extremely vulnerable (an abandoned covid shielder), we cannot go & demonstrate, so were also shouted at by supposed allies who refuse to get disabilities & want us backing their chants while they systematically refuse to have our back. its knackering to have had to have yr own back since childhood. in increasingly authoritarian times we gotta remember the fragile-won nature ov victories, stop the removal ov our language, we need our languagings, our language-sings. those still in drowning street brought in clause 28, & they're always itchy over who to target next, yet so many have undermined, subverted n slow-toppled that grubby wee erection ov politicians n power who need-&-greed an enemy (any, & then the next) to justify why its not milk&honey quite yet ... oppositional defiance is querying & queerying, bisexualities break binary.
madnesses are armour against the onslaught. lets 'rewrite the future' - theres always multiple possibilities. to dissent effectively, don't meet 'em head-on but do it on the cuuurve as us bi's do. bisexualities messinesses are essential ingredient in undermining systems. these increasingly authoritarian times destabilise & destroy minds, communities & solidarities so lets build bridges nae walls. more oppositional defiance is needed & bisexualities are acts ov dissent

burn / gobscure are donating their fee for this article to: https://opencollective.com/transtechtent
The Trans Tech Tent is an organisation based out ov South Wales helping the trans community to participate online, study, and reach their potential.

Out of Mind, Out of Sight – Ellie Page

There's an episode of *Buffy* that has haunted me for years. In the months leading up to my inpatient admission, I found myself thinking about it every day, particularly as my list of physical health conditions continued to spiral into absurdity. In this particular episode, a girl is so ignored and so unseen that she starts to become invisible. Anti-realist theories of 'reality' are provided as an explanation, namely that reality is created only by and within our perception; the girl was never looked at by anyone. No one perceived her actually being there, and so she ceased to be visible.

No wonder she's miffed.

At the end, some secret service personnel take her away, wrapped in a red school theatre curtain, to join a school of thousands of teenagers whom this has happened to, and that the government trains as spies. Thankfully my so-called 'delusions' didn't reach as far as the FBI assassin academy.

***

"This wasn't a great power that she could control. This was something that was done to her. That we did to her.'

I had extremely severe endometriosis from a very young age (13) and had undergone what turned out to be far too many surgical attempts to remove it. I had this physical condition throughout my young adult life as well, but until the age of 25 did not identify as 'disabled' because, in many ways, I wasn't. I had a quite severe and complicated long-term health condition that interrupted my life sporadically, through 'flares'. I could walk about freely and do pretty much everything my non-disabled friends could do (apart from give birth, probably). I started having problems with my hips a few years before my admission to Pentagon Limbo (mental health ward), but again, my treatment of steroid injections meant that the issues only affected me episodically rather than constantly hampering my mobility. In the year leading up to my admission at Limbo, I had gone through so much stress that I had killed off a little part of my brain, causing me to develop narcolepsy, atypical cataplexy and atypical migraines, as well as a severe sleep REM behaviour disorder. In addition to this, my hip treatment had stopped working. It was a period of a few months that transitioned me from being someone who was relatively popular, worked on their feet for 50+ hours a week, socialised every single evening and studied a Masters alongside that, to being someone who couldn't get from their bed up the stairs to the bathroom, never went out and had to stop the job that they loved. I was in a constant state of discomfort at best, and severe pain and immobility at worst. Mentally, I struggled with this new identity and I believe this, along with feeling a complete and total loss of any sexuality, is what led to my admission.

I knew from a young age that I would not be able to give birth. My cervix eroded when I was 16 and by age 17, they had decided to operate on what they found by accident: Stage 4 recto-vaginal endometriosis & adenomyosis, as well as a cervical cancer scare that took a while and some more surgery to fix. I used to not tell people about my health problems, largely because they were centred around gynaecology, which means vaginas, which means people feeling uncomfortable when you talk to them, and me feeling embarrassed and judged when having to explain what was wrong. It felt like I couldn't have a conversation about my health without mentioning my womb, which, to me, was basically like talking to someone about your genitals. When I was younger, people assumed that any abnormality to do with your boobs or your fanny was something to do with having lots of unprotected sex with lots of people and therefore A) your fault and B) made you repulsive and disease-ridden. I remember being asked by partners more than once - and this goes on into adulthood - 'Well, is it safe or can I catch it? What will happen if I catch it?'

This stupid disease ruined my social life, confidence, grades, mental health, finances, intellectual capacity, my degree, everything. I loathed it. It was always there, separating me from wherever it was I wanted to fit in with. The thing I cared about the absolute least was the first and only thing people would ask me about: my fertility. Of course, this only happened if we had managed to get the conversation as far as me saying what was wrong, and if they hadn't already assumed I was a sex maniac riddled with STDs and run a bazillion miles away.

The sympathetic look always came first: 'Oh, does that mean you can't have kids?'
 'No.'
 'Oh, so you can have kids?' Raised eyebrows and happiness.
 'Well, of course I can. I can adopt and foster, which is what I've always wanted to do.'
Eyebrows down, the pity look returning: 'Oh, so you can't have your own kids.'
 'They would be my own kids.'
 'But I mean you couldn't have them yourself.'
 'I probably can't get pregnant and give birth, no, but I don't want to, so it's fine.'
 'What about in the future, though?'
 'I just said I'll adopt.'
 'Men can be funny about that you know.'
 'Why are you assuming I'm straight?'

'Oh, sorry. I didn't realise you were gay, you should have just said! Then I wouldn't have kept asking about the baby stuff!'

'I'm not gay, I'm bi, and my sexuality has nothing to do with whether or not I want or will have kids. I can be gay and want to adopt, and actually I can be gay and want to get pregnant and give birth.'

Well, by this point, a look of slight fear usually penetrated the pity gaze as they assumed I had some kind of infertility-related delusion which causes inappropriate defensiveness and insanity on the topic of children and babies.

My sexuality, like my infertility, had nothing to do with whether or not I wanted or would have kids. That was what I'd thought.

But I was wrong about this, apparently. Since I realised that 'gay' and 'bi' and 'straight' were all just social constructs (this happened whilst I was off sick with a horrendous fever aged 14 and watching *Brokeback Mountain* for the first time), I had always known that my sexuality was what others would describe as "bi'," i.e. sometimes I fancied people and sometimes they were of different genders. This just seemed obvious, natural and uninteresting to me, not an identity label or talking point. I actually believed that this was true of everyone, but that people just didn't admit it. My deep secret throughout my teenage years was that I was desperate to be male. Absolutely desperate, I would have done anything to be reborn as a male. In this life that I believed I was 'supposed' to be born into, I was talented at singing and dancing and lived as a handsome bisexual man who was a musical theatre star in the West End. A story for another time, perhaps.

Let's flash forward to the year I had to take out of university in order to attend to a variety of surgical exploits. I remember coming home drunk after a standard weekday pub night with my housemate who ran a coffee shop.

129

I don't know how it came up, but he was like 'Oh, I didn't realise you were bi! Have you always been bi?'
I was like 'Well, it's not exactly something you come out as, you know, like if you were gay and everyone had assumed you were straight.'
He said that it could be, and that he had a bisexual friend who came out in a similar way to the 'closet' trope.
 'Oh… in that case, tonight was my coming out party! Woohoo!'
 I then started cartwheeling about, making us have extra celebrations as part of what I retrospectively declared to be my coming out party.

***

It wasn't only cis-women who assumed that my biggest concern regarding my health was my fertility. It was also, it turns out, the ONLY concern of the NHS and all medical practitioners I came into contact with. Despite it being glaringly obvious that I was infertile, my adult life would be spent trying to convince every medical practitioner I came into contact with that I DO NOT WANT TO GIVE BIRTH.

Through trial and error, I realised that as part of this scheme, there were various aspects of my identity that I could not share. I would never receive appropriate treatment for my various gynaecological traumas if I continued trying to explain the actual situation, which was that I couldn't think of anything worse than carrying and giving birth to a baby, but that I do want to adopt or foster kids. Turns out this would give me a tick next to 'Wants to have children', and I would be even further from what they and I knew to be the only treatment that might stand a chance of improving things: a full or partial hysterectomy.

I thought it might help my case if I told them I was bisexual. Big mistake. Unfortunately, this word has a totally different meaning in the context of biomedical practice. Apparently it translates as 'hyper sexual', 'indecisive,' 'straight but being difficult,' 'manic' and 'mentally ill'. This turned out to open a whole different can of inappropriate-question-worms that I hadn't previously encountered during my routine appointments. Doctors and nurses now wanted to know about my recreational drug use, contraception and how frequently I was tested for STDs, how many people I was having sex with currently, whether I was on any mental health medication and if I was taking it properly.

Well, that put me back several paces in terms of the respect and autonomy I had spent years trying desperately to build amongst the plethora of professionals involved in my care. Big, unexpected blow to the dignity wagon there. I was being assessed in these appointments in entirely new ways as if I was someone who constantly eats used needles and refuses to take their medication. But I wasn't any of these perfectly acceptable things. I was exactly the same person I'd been the last time I saw them, back when they thought I was straight and apparently 'therefore' not a steaming, walking incubator of STDs.

Right around this bizarre stage of my ever-thwarted 'Get the Doctors to Listen to Me' campaign is when I ended up as an inpatient on a psychiatric ward.

***

Sometimes, you run out of battery.

Someone from the mental health team came to see me in my house-share at around midday on a Friday. This was after I had taken an overdose of my prescription meds the night before and curled up to become invisible in a cocoon underneath a church bench. She suggested that an in-patient admission. She left.

I sat on my bed, too scared to move, just staring at the wall for some time. It was finally happening. I had worked for years in youth work and social care. I had just spent a year working on an acute adult mental health ward, running art therapy groups. I'd always had this phobia that at some point in my professional career, I would get 'found out' as a mad person. That the closet doors would be sprung open in the spotlight, to reveal me for what I really am: a person with psychiatric diagnoses and a history of mental and physical trauma. These are things that carry with them a stigma that renders me categorically incapable of carrying out professional duties, particularly within the sphere of public health and community care. I feared bumping into someone that I worked with whenever I went to one of my own psychiatric appointments or therapy sessions. I had excuses prepared before I got to the building: 'Right, who is it most likely I will bump into? What is a realistic and believable excuse for me being here professionally?'

There was a shame and sadness that accompanied these preparatory paranoia sessions. I firmly believe that people can have 'significant mental health issues' and maintain high quality and fantastic lives, careers and friendships. There are social approaches to mental health which regard experiences that are usually deemed' psychosis' as perfectly reasonable responses to the various ways in which we understand and exist in the world. I always felt somewhat disgusted with myself that I, a passionate advocate for the hearing voices approach, was becoming part of the problem by not taking a stand and sharing my lived experience (or at least the fact that I had it) with colleagues and by consequently allowing it to be associated with a sense of shame.

I phoned her to voice my concerns about bumping into people I knew at the hospital, especially someone I had had to report to the police a number of times that week, who had triggered part of my PTSD. She reassured me, 'No, no, you'll be going to a female-only ward. It's a really nice and quiet ward, so you don't have to worry about bumping into him.' A dark veil lifted as I imagined that perhaps this wouldn't be awful, but instead a quite wholesome experience that might actually allow me the time I needed to rest and feel better. We agreed that I would pack a bag and get a taxi to the central hospital, and that from there they would accompany me in an ambulance to a different mental health hospital. I can barely remember packing or getting to the central hospital, but I did. I had to wait in the waiting room for a very long time, without being seen or spoken to. I never saw the woman who had visited me, but eventually I was told by a random staff member to get in this cab which would take me where I needed to be. They didn't tell me where I was going. I arrived and walked totally disorientated and disassociated into the reception. I couldn't believe no one had come with me. I didn't know how I was going to be able to speak. I didn't know if people could even see me.

But then the reception gave me a filthy look. 'What is it? Are you staying here?'

'Ellie Page.' I whispered very hoarsely, scared of the sound of my own voice. 'Erm… I'm supposed to be admitted.'

'Huh? Has noone come with you? Well, who told you you were staying here?'

'Social worker at hospital,' I tried to croak, tears welling up.

'Well, no one told me you were coming. Who knows you're here?'

I completely shut down, mouth tight, tears starting to roll quietly. I wasn't exactly in the mental state to circumnavigate an administrative comedy of errors.

I've realised whilst writing this that the fear wasn't so much that I was just turning physiologically invisible but that I really felt that I was at the start of ceasing to exist. Turning up at an austere mental health hospital having been driven there by a male stranger who didn't speak, only to be not expected by anyone there, and for no one to have any idea or record of who I am, did nothing to ease the feeling that I was about to fade away. The paper trail of my existence on this planet had already started to be erased.

So, I just stood there, so disassociated that I didn't even exist mentally. I apparently gave my name, date of birth, the hospital I was sent from. I clutched my dressing gown, sure that my particles had started disintegrating, along with any evidence that I had ever been on the planet.

Eventually someone came down and said accusatively at me 'Well, who said you could come here?' I think I just cried. I don't really remember much else, other than when we went past the sign to the women's ward.

'Wait, wait, they promised me it was going to be a women's-only ward?' My mind and voice had come back to my body enough to whisper-challenge what was happening. 'I know a guy on the mixed ward, I'm only here because they said I wouldn't be on a ward with him.' 'Well, there's no beds free on the women's ward, so you were never going there.' I was shown to a large empty room with an extremely low camp-bed in it, bars on the windows, blood and shit stains crusted into the floors and walls.

I felt a bit calmer as a realisation dawned on me. 'Ah. This must be limbo,' I realised. 'I've stopped existing. I'm being held here while I await judgement, or whatever happens next.'

***

Competition for staff attention on an inpatient mental health ward is seriously fucking fierce. Like, you have to be doing something really insane or that really impedes on someone's safeguarding responsibility or fag break for them to actually notice that you exist.

After nearly 2 weeks, I was taken to an appointment with a psychiatrist who looked like he hated me, the world and all humans who weren't him. Especially the women humans, and the young women humans in particular. It's just a vibe you get, when you walk into a room and everyone in there has made their mind up about you before you've even sat down. There are certain men, in particular, who you just know when you meet them, hate you just for who you are. They hate every visible aspect of your identity and make some more up for good measure. The most hated part of your identity, the one they can deduce from the moment they look at you, is your gender situation. If they deduce female, they hate you. If they can't assign you a binary gender from your presentation, they hate you. The other aspects they dislike are pinpointed at the cross-section of your intelligence and political leanings. From this, they are able to assume your perspective on psychology as an institution, and on psychiatrists.

I remember so clearly sitting in this room with the psychiatrist and a nurse as I was asked what my symptoms were now and how my treatment had been.
'What treatment?' I explained that since I was checked in by a nice on-call GP and her clipboard, no one had spoken to me.
'What do you mean no one has spoken to you?'

'Well, I have been here for two weeks, and no one has come to check on me or have a chat with me. I've just been ignored.'

He snorted slightly and looked over his glasses at me. 'Well? What on earth did you expect?'

I was flummoxed.

'What, you think your nurse is just going to come in for chats?'

He was laughing at me but without cracking a smile. 'Why are you even here?'

Right there, in that moment, I had no idea if I was even really there at all, let alone why I was there. I felt simultaneously excruciatingly, nakedly visible, and like I was slowly fading into nothingness. The last people who would ever see me would be this guy and the nurse, I thought. They can barely see me enough to know that I exist, let alone remember me if I disappear.

It shocked me, for some reason, that the psychiatrist was so openly comfortable with me being ignored by staff whilst enduring a period of hospitalisation for a mental health crisis. Not only comfortable, but he actually thought it laughable that I expected as much attention as a chat from staff during the two-week period of my stay.

***

While in limbo, I had spent ages doodling the same phrase I found in a Dalai Lama book of quotes that for some reason I had with me. I've just gone to look back at the poem, to make sure that I could quote it directly:

As long as space endures,
as long as sentient beings remain,
until then, may I too remain

Turns out I missed out the final line of the stanza while I was repeating it in my notebook on the ward:

and dispel the miseries of the world.

Forget your troubles but not your sins

Ellie Page

WE KNOW THAT QUEERNESS IS NO LONGER SEEN AS A MENTAL ILLNESS BUT WE WILL STILL FUCK YOU OVER WITH A PERSONALITY DISORDER LABEL

13

There's No Sense to Be Made in The UK Mental Healthcare System – Artie Carden

1.

    I have a long relationship with NHS mental health services. I have really struggled with my mental wellbeing for the majority of my life, and my first trip to the GP to talk about it at age 13 or 14 set the tone for many appointments with NHS mental health services to come.

I still vividly remember this appointment. I struggled to express how I felt. I just knew my deep sadness and hopelessness weren't 'normal', or were a warning sign. Feeling like I couldn't organically express how I was feeling led to years of self-harm. In some ways, it was lucky (?) I had some physical 'evidence' of my inner turmoil because this GP spoke down to me like a child; she just didn't believe how empty but full of negative emotions I was until I pulled up my sleeves.

Even when she saw my red raw forearms with no space left unharmed, her tone remained condescending: 'Oh, that looks like it hurts.'

Well, yes, Gladys*, obviously it hurts. While this next line is going to sound dramatic, I still stand by this: it doesn't hurt as much as how I am feeling. What I can see now as an adult in my 20s who has done a lot of self-reflection in these last 15 years is that it's the autism again! And the ADHD a little too. But that's a story for another time.

It was worth it because I am still here, and I never saw that GP again. I went to my first NHS counselling under CAHMS. Pause for a long sigh. The first counsellor I had wasn't the best fit, but she wasn't dreadful. It was talking therapy and Jenna* encouraged me to bring in drawings I'd made (my second-best form of self-expression). At this point, I was so distressed and traumatised that I was experiencing psychosis. I'd become so fractured in my sense of self, I felt like I wasn't even experiencing my entire life as me. As a narrative lover, I will add this is foreshadowing.

My gender and sexuality never really entered the picture with my counsellors for years because I didn't feel shame or conflict within myself about being queer. All my romantic and sexual relationships were with cis (at the time) boys/men until I went to university at age 20.

I do feel like this was a failure on the part of many counsellors I had as I'd never been made to feel like it was safe to talk about queerness or gender. Counselling did give me a space to process my thoughts and emotions and practice wording them –talking about them, even identifying them in some respects.

I don't remember how long I saw Jenna. It felt like months but I had to move onto a new counsellor as Jenna went on maternity leave. The next woman I saw was Clare,* who was very different to Jenna.

Jenna was pretty good at being a blank slate but that also meant I never really experienced any warmth from her either. I thought I was going to like Clare. But that was the only session I had with her. It was a review session though she was a total stranger. She told me she thought I was better now and should be discharged.

This shocked me. I felt like I'd maybe just gotten comfortable talking about anything at all as Jenna had gotten to know me, my experiences and how I think. Here was this stranger telling me I was 'better' when I had started attempting suicide within the same year; I was still self-harming so much I'd moved to other body parts and other types of self-harm, as well as disordered eating behaviours. I had some things I still wanted to talk through and told Clare as much.

'That was in the past. Nothing will change what's happened,' she told me.

After hearing that, I knew I didn't want to keep seeing Clare and I let her discharge me from the service.

2.

This was the beginning of my two years of suicide attempts in secret in my room alone at night. It is near impossible to talk through suicidal feelings without triggering a fight or flight response in your counsellor especially when you're under the age of 18. Struggling with friendships, romantic and sexual relationships and problems with my schoolwork, I felt like I had no one to turn to about anything. I had been starving and restricting for months. I was at my most suicidal because I understood myself the least in an inherently abusive society.

I had a lot of stuff I needed to work through, not many options and not much choice. You get who you get in the NHS, it's a total lottery: 6 to 12 sessions. You can't make requests, or you're seen as ungrateful.

I started seeing my school's counsellor, Gwen*, who was much better to talk to. She had wild, curly, dyed-red hair, was non-judgmental but also had a human response.

It helped I got to ditch a class every week to see her. I wish there could have been more signs I could talk about LGBTQ+ topics with her. I don't know how able school staff would have been; growing up in the first decade of the 2000s was horrific. Whilst section 28 had been out ruled in 2003, the effects continued for a long, long time. There were rumours about which of our teachers were gay, but they couldn't be out. It was revolutionary that my Personal Social Health and Economics teacher talked about a variety of contraception in our sex-ed class, including femidoms and dental dams, and showed us a documentary on trans people. I still sing this woman's praises for making a really awkward class, funny and enjoyable as well as actually educational.

I don't know how much was in my teachers and school staff's control with regards to having leaflets with LGBTQ+ info or posters to tell you the counselling was a safe space... but if they were there, I like to think I might have talked more about it to explore the words I had at the time and what I was feeling. Over half of LGBTQ+ young people don't feel like there is a safe adult to talk to or confide in within school about LGBTQ+ related topics.[2] I hid a lot of my queerness from counsellors because it was risky to talk about them. The only gays I remember on TV were from *Skins*, which was a show romanticising self-destruction rather than seeking help.

I experimented with my sense of style and how I presented myself and people started to comment that I was 'one of the boys' or butch. This proceeded into my time at college.

---

[2] All statistics and references on this page are from this article by Stonewall:
https://www.stonewall.org.uk/experiences-lgbtq-children-and-young-people

Nearly half of queer teenagers, and 64% of trans young people, are bullied for being queer or trans in school. This can also be less about you actually being out as queer or trans, and more about the perception the people targeting you have. If you look or act a certain way, you are a target for homophobic abuse. I feel very lucky to have never experienced shame around my gender or sexuality. The targeted harassment I experienced for it didn't upset me at all. There was still plenty I would have benefitted from talking about.

I wish I could have used my counselling as a space to talk through the shame and embarrassment sewn into the slurs being thrown around at people. When I was in school, gay was an insult. The f-slur would be thrown about between boys, and 'dyke' and 'lesbian' were whispered in the changing rooms like dirty words. Nearly half of queer and trans people in sixth-form colleges regularly hear homophobic language.

3.

Moving into college is where I made queer friends. I don't think I was able to access any mental health support at this time. I think I could have really used counselling or talking therapy, but I don't think there was an on-site counsellor. I was so low and distressed; my self-harm had amped up and so had my suicidal thoughts. My last attempt was in late January 2012. I had lost a couple of friendships with people I cared about a lot, people I considered my best friends, and I had no one to talk to about it. I felt ashamed and worthless.

Sometimes I second-guessed if I was bi because I'd only dated or slept with boys. My queer friends would take our one straight friend to gay bars in the city, but never extended an invitation to me.

Not being able to talk to a counsellor about how isolated I felt ruined me. There were so many layers to my isolation that I am still unpicking now. I learned repeatedly that being 'too much' got me ditched. If I complained too much, if I had too much excitement or passion, if I was too happy for my accomplishments, if I was too queer or trans… I was a snob, I was arrogant, I was annoying, I was weird. Everyone else was allowed to do these things.

Now I know that much of this was my ADHD and autism; things that make me innately me, just like my queerness and transness… people have been taught to reject those characteristics. I was taught to reject those characteristics by society.

I have slowly peeled away layers of trauma and societal expectations to find my true self. It has been rough. I was not always helped by my counsellors. Being so many marginalised identities has made it hard to make friends, fall in love, find community… find the right mental healthcare.

No one is versed in 'how to be sensitive to oppressed communities,' even counsellors and therapists. I mirrored everyone I'd ever been around because I'd been taught no one liked me (the real me) so I buried that person so deep. I'd do anything to be friends with someone and got caught in many bad situations where I was lucky I got out relatively unscathed. I was just this vessel with nothing inside but sadness, anger and trauma.

A few months before I attended university at age 20, I saw a counsellor called Joan.* She was a lovely lady who was invested in helping provide a space for me to talk and build a foundation to fall back on when our 12 sessions were up to prepare me for university.

I'd worked out towards the end that my feelings didn't line up with my assigned gender. I remember wearing my first binder to one of my sessions. I didn't have a 'new name' yet. I felt like I needed a new name to be this new person, which isn't true. The name did come eventually. But I still went by my legal name.

First, I came out to my mum. Then I half came out to my gran; I didn't think she would get the gender thing. I cut my hair. Joan had helped me put together a document of warning signs, affirmations and a toolbox of things to do if I started spiralling again. The most solid help I'd ever been provided at that time.

4.

At university, I was reliving my teen years the way I wished they could have been. I got to dress how I felt best. I got to enjoy queer events with my queer friends and study a subject I loved. I was having my first queer relationship and it was intense, traumatic (we really went through it together) and amazing. We were both working out who we were and what we wanted. I can thank them for what they brought to my life, but I had started experiencing high anxiety and psychosis again.

The high stress I was dealing with from my relationship had led me to revert to old protective measures. I wasn't myself at times, and constantly in a state of dissociation. I told the counsellor I was seeing through a local mental health charity that I felt like my personality had fractured: I wasn't experiencing life as myself; it was more like fragments of myself. It's only now as I feel like I am slowly healing that the fragments have glued themselves back together. I have picked up a few of the missing pieces I didn't even have back then.

I think this counsellor, Sarah*, was the first person I talked to more explicitly about being queer. Sarah struggled to keep up because people I talked about used the same pronouns as each other or neutral pronouns, and she couldn't tell one person from another. That was quite frustrating. I think once you have gotten used to talking to and about queer people, you are versed in a new language. Counsellors often lack fluency. I had to spoon-feed a lot of info, which slowed things down because I wasn't going to misgender anyone to make it easier. When my sessions came to an end, I wasn't done but I knew it was coming.

It's weird and feels quite dysfunctional but a lot of counsellors plan out the 6-12 sessions for you. They make all the decisions about how to get the most out of it. You can't deviate from the plan, or you set things back.

A part of my queer identity I hadn't been able to explore or discuss much is my asexuality. I had a moment in university where I identified asexuality was a thing and I related to some of the traits and experiences, but something made me push it to one side. I think this was more confusing to grasp than my gender or bisexuality because it didn't all fit and I'd not heard anyone talk about it in more detail or with nuance. I was sex-shamed and infantilised by my teenage friends for being 'vanilla' or 'frigid' or not magically knowing how to do sex because I had no interest in porn. In university, I'd been able to talk more openly about sex in general with my friends, but certain conversations would leave me feeling like I couldn't relate to anyone. Even with my friends on the ace spectrum I wasn't sure how to have the conversation. Everything I felt was brushed off with 'everyone feels this,' which is something I've heard a lot as a disabled and neurodivergent person.

I wish there was more of an accessible way to discuss compulsory heterosexuality (comp-het) and how that can still impact you as a queer trans person. From the spectrum of asexuality, to platonic life partners, to non-monogamous relationships... I knew I wouldn't find answers with the counsellors I'd been seeing over the years and I've never had queer-centred counselling support. I've gotten used to talking about taboo subjects with people, but part of my experience with asexuality is that I'm uncomfortable talking about sex in graphic detail as I experience some sex-repulsion and sex trauma. I was too ashamed of sex and feeling dirty or gross after sex with people... it felt more like a me problem than a societal problem with sex. But it's always society.

5.

My last experience of NHS services before I entered private therapy was when I'd been home after graduating from university for a year before the pandemic began.

I was feeling very low. I wasn't processing any of my physical health issues. I just wanted to talk to someone. When the lady on the phone found out I was diagnosed with borderline personality disorder (BPD or EUPD), she was extremely hesitant to put me into talking therapy as they recommend a different kind of care for people with BPD. This care isn't provided in the area I'm in. It is just non-existent. I had to convince her to allow me to be put on the waitlist. I didn't want help for my BPD; I just wanted a space to talk to someone about my physical health. She agreed, telling me I'd 'redeemed' people with BPD in her eyes. She thought people couldn't 'get better' from BPD...

I felt very slimy after that phone call. Refusing to help people because of a diagnosis when they reach out for help is disgusting. What if I had been bereaved and was seeking grief counselling? Would I be refused because I have BPD and they think I should go to specialist dialectical behaviour therapy for BPD when someone in my life has died? There's no sense to be made in the UK mental healthcare system.

I have gone to a psychologist or psychiatrist for a diagnostic assessment three times. Often, I've been left with more questions than I came with or been put at risk by their actions. As a teenager, I was diagnosed with anxiety/depression with 'signs of' a personality disorder. This led me to another search for a diagnosis (BPD) years later with the help of some university staff and a very nice diagnostician.

My most recent attempt has been for my ADHD diagnosis. I wasn't sure how I felt about Ray*, this psychiatrist who'd swing between being calming and supportive, and dismissive and cold. He asked my gender, a question I hadn't expected to be asked. The wording of this and the fact that the service wasn't technically NHS made me feel like it would *maybe* be okay to say 'I don't really identify with gender at all.' Then he asked me my pronouns, which I provided with a disclaimer that they could use she/her to avoid confusing other doctors who may be reading the report.

'But thank you for asking, though,' I said.

'Well, we have to, or some people might get offended.'

I'd made a mistake.

149

A month later, it was all in the report under 'Psychiatric history'. Not even 'General patient history' a little further down. 'Psychiatric history.' The report was already on the NHS system waiting to be read by my GP... I'm chronically ill and have a large and varied team of doctors taking care of me. I was not out to any of them. *Nothing can undo this* was my fast realisation. The responses from friends and family were mostly along the lines of 'What?' 'Surely they can't do that?' 'Isn't that unethical?' And whilst I agree and think it would have been nice to double-check with me before pasting that on my permanent NHS record anyone can access, I don't know if they have broken any rules. Which sucks.

Whilst I have become more and more open to mentioning my queerness to doctors, including mental health doctors, it hasn't been the same with my transness. I have never mentioned this to any counsellor or therapist except this ADHD diagnostician and my private trauma therapist. And treatment like this explains why. It has been made clear to me that I will face a lot less active abuse/neglect if I mention being queer to any degree than if I mention being trans, especially with the anti-trans rhetoric being so heightened in the UK right now.

I think my physical appearance codes me as queer and more people can comprehend queerness. Most people can understand being in love with someone, even if not in a queer sense.

I've talked about my girlfriends, partners and boyfriends all at once with different professionals since I entered my twenties with barely an eyebrow being raised.

Gender, especially a gender that isn't easy to explain or understand, is a different story. As the ADHD psychiatrist's response shows, it's considered a symptom of something that needs 'fixing'. Anyone might find it hard to explain something so abstract without signalling mental instability… but as an autistic struggling with alexithymia, which is specifically around my feelings[3], it has been so difficult.

I didn't talk about gender until I was with someone who I felt wouldn't be alarmed or think I was unwell. I recently heard the saying 'feelings come before words'. Words are a very limited way of explaining an experience you are having.

A big part of my personal journey has been about validating feelings I had in the past because as a child, I was often failed by the system even though I was reaching out for help.

When I write about my thoughts and experiences today, I use statistics to help illustrate my points. A lot of those statistics I never used to see: they're about things that were never investigated when I was under 20. Things like:

- Nearly half of disabled LGBTQ+ young people have tried to take their own life. The rates are also extremely high for trans (40%), non-binary (33%) and queer (20%) young people.[4]
- Disabled LGBTQ+ teenagers are more likely to self-harm (80%) than LGBTQ+ young people who aren't

---

[3] Alexithymia is a broad term for problems with identifying and describing emotions

[4] https://www.stonewall.org.uk/experiences-lgbtq-children-and-young-people

disabled (64%)[5] and non-disabled cisgender heterosexual teenagers.[6]
- Girls** with ADHD are more likely to develop anxiety and depression than girl without ADHD. They are also more likely to attempt suicide or self-harm.[7]
- Children with ADHD hear more criticism than non-ADHD children do and they are told they have no 'reason' for their struggle.

Looking at the statistics now available to us is depressing but also extremely validating. The way our society functions in the UK, mental illness is inevitable for a marginalised person, especially a multiply-marginalised person. It's hard giving feedback and suggestions on how to improve the mental health system because we can't fix the mental health system without fixing the flaws of British society.

Not every counsellor will be right for every patient that comes through the door. If we don't have easier access to queer therapists and counsellors, we need better and more diverse training around sexuality and gender. We also can't forget the barriers for marginalised people who want to become counsellors, therapists and doctors even though they would be the best people to serve their own communities. I see it from a physical health point of view and a mental health one.

---

[5] https://www.stonewall.org.uk/experiences-lgbtq-children-and-young-people

[6] https://sites.manchester.ac.uk/carms/2020/10/06/why-is-the-lgbtq-community-disproportionately-affected-by-mental-health-problems-and-suicide/#_edn12

[7] https://www.ncbi.nlm.nih.gov/pmc/articles/PMC3543865/

Doing therapy with a disabled woman who focuses on a holistic and trauma-informed route has changed my life. She had heard me for exactly who I am. She has heard me for my queerness, my asexuality, my transness and with all my disabilities (including ADHD and autism) without judgement or poor ignorant advice. She's helped me heal traumas that disrupted my healthcare and my daily life whilst giving me the space to explore all these things. All this has helped me heal my inner child who didn't get the care they needed or the representation they deserved. Now it's time for the dejected teenagers in all of us, the ones who were messed up by the systems in place, to step forward and make change.

*names changed, obviously. **'girls has an asterisk as it is bio-essentialist and binary-centric

14

DIAGNOSTIC DYSPHORIA – LJ Cooper

I was assigned female at birth, Schizophrenic at twenty, Personality Disordered at twenty-two. At twenty-four I (re)assigned myself Mad, Neurodivergent and Agender (I wish it was as simple as that). I'm thirty-one now. I first encountered psychiatric services at the age of seventeen and spent seven years in and out of both hospital and the so-called criminal justice system before learning how to stay out of trouble. I don't think I got "better"; I behaved myself and the space away from mental health services, and time out of crisis, was what I needed to find other ways to be in the world. This essay is about some of those ways.

Psychiatric diagnosis and gender have a lot in common: they both were done *to* me, they are both very hard to shake off once assigned, they are both product and mechanism of white supremacy and a white settler colonial patriarchy, and my experience of them is decided by other intersecting things including race, ethnicity, class, sexuality. Both are a powerful force that has irreparably shaped my life and how I can move through the world, how I experience myself and my body. They police and restrict. They are also not separate from each other – psychiatric diagnoses are gendered, and gender, when it is not experienced or performed correctly, has its own set of diagnostic categories.

I've known I was queer since I was a teenager, but my priority at school was fitting in and acting like everyone else: *Just Be Normal*. Still, I drunkenly kissed girls at parties; there was drama and loss navigated via MSN messenger.

I felt a gnawing discomfort at being seen as a girl, and I gravitated towards my soft butch GCSE English teacher in a way I couldn't explain but I suspect was about, for the first time, seeing someone who I wanted to be.

My parents never suggested being gay was a problem. But I grew up in the shadow of Section 28 which was only repealed when I was twelve, in 2003. This legislation banned 'the promotion of homosexuality' by the local authorities who were in charge of most state schools in England. It meant that being gay (let alone any other kind of queer) felt like it should be a secret, and there was a sense that talking about it was illegal – those moments where teachers would shake their heads and explain: 'I can't talk about that.' Once I was in mental health services, my sexuality became problematic, unwieldly, dangerous – read through the lens of my diagnosis.

So over the years I put it away, I put it all away. I felt that they were able to take away all sorts of things from me (turn meaningful voices and experiences into symptoms, diagnose my personality, who I was, as the issue) but I was going to hold onto my queerness. I wasn't going to let them make that another problem with me.

Borderline Personality Disorder (BPD) is also called Emotionally Unstable Personality Disorder (EUPD). It has a very broad set of diagnostic criteria but is often a label given to women who are difficult, who have experienced trauma, who self-harm or try to complete suicide. This essay isn't about the problems with BPD more broadly as a diagnosis (although I will say that I think it does more harm than good). Instead, I want to reflect on one part of the diagnostic criteria: 'You don't have a strong sense of who you are, and it can change significantly depending on who you're with.'[8]

---

[8] From the Mind website.

No one told me I was diagnosed with BPD. I'd shrugged and agreed to move my care over to the Complex Cases Service (later renamed the Personality Disorder Pathway) after having been with the Early Intervention in Psychosis service far past their two-year limit. I'd met with the psychiatrist in the service as an outpatient. I'd sat on the waiting list passively. I'd pursued Dialectical Behaviour Therapy (DBT) because it apparently helped people who hurt themselves like I did, who were living in a chaotic storm of blue lights and holding on by their fingertips to survive.

Then I was in hospital again, in early 2014, moving through the acute wards as usual, and my attempts to hurt myself became "unmanageable".

One day I was escorted across the hospital grounds and through several sets of doors, into a room on Springbank Ward, one of two specialist personality disorder wards in the NHS. A female-only ward with twelve beds. I don't know what the ward is like now, but back then it was chronically understaffed, underserved, and total chaos. The month and a bit I spent there was some of the most traumatic time I spent in hospital.

I knew then that any uncertainty I experienced around my gender would be read through the lens of a personality disorder.

Several years before, in 2011, I'd watched the Channel 4 show *My Transsexual Summer,* drawn to it in the same inexplicable and unavoidable way I'd been drawn to my GCSE English teacher. Though I have no idea how the show's framing and narration would measure up to a critical viewing, what stood out to me were the previously unconsidered possibilities around gender that I watched play out on screen.

Shortly afterwards I bought my first binder and joined a FTM (female to male, an acronym sometimes used for transmen) chatroom. This wasn't something I shared with anyone – I didn't even know what it meant. What I did know is that if I brought it up in a psychiatric context, it would become another thing wrong with me. Gender Dysphoria is, after all, another diagnosis. When nurses asked me why I was so unhappy on Springbank, I could give them plenty of reasons. An additional one, silent in the background, was my deep discomfort with being on a ward for women.

BPD made it a problem that my identity was fluid, changeable, difficult to pin down. I realised the only way to solve this was to 'fix' my identity, pin it to a board. The last five years out of psychiatric services has felt a bit like trying to unstick all the parts of me I made rigid in order to survive; I was controlling, inflexible, didn't feel like I could afford to be spontaneous (impulsive), felt like I had to be one thing to all people, tried to write a single story of my life, of my time in hospital. That last one was really where it came undone.

Trying to translate my experiences of madness into a story for my peer support worker training (I ended up in the 'long term service user' to 'peer support worker' pipeline at my trust) made me feel deeply unhappy. I felt like I was trying to fit a square peg into a round hole.

It was around this time I first started reading comics and zines[9] which offered a new way of thinking about, talking about, and telling a 'story' of, madness. At the same time, I was doing Open University modules that discussed the history of the service user movement, of Mad Pride, of 'Recovery' not as some objective thing, but as a model, one way of thinking about mental health.

---

[9] Zines are DIY, self-published booklets, pamphlets, magazines – I make them, I read a lot of them, and these days I research and write about them.

I found a new way to describe myself: Neurodivergent and Mad. I decided that, so long as I could help it, I wouldn't allow myself and my experiences to be written by doctors and nurses in medical terms. Whilst 'Recovery' expected me to be at the end of a journey, the other side of something, I still felt like I was stuck in-between. Gloria Anzaldúa (1942-2004) writes of and from the Borderland – of the power and potential to be found there. Anzaldúa's writing is situated in the geographical Mexico/US borderlands, and it's important not to abstract her words and lose that location, with its lived realities and injustices.

But Anzaldúa also writes of psychological, sexual and spiritual borderlands, and she identifies queerness as a kind of borderland, as another way to occupy the borderland, in conversation with all the others. It was the first time that I'd seen being in-between being described as something creative, powerful, magical, transformative, with a radical potential.

It's not a coincidence that this comes from a postcolonial context. The in-between threatens the binaries that sustain white settler colonial patriarchy, which is why its inhabitants are so heavily policed, experience violence, allowed only to be one thing or the other: American/Mexican, boy/girl, sane/mad.

Three months out of Springbank, I was in my first long-term relationship with someone I'd met on OkCupid. We moved in together pretty much immediately (which worked out ok; we're still living together now, in a civil partnership, nine years later).

Unlike me, Abi had been confident and vocal about her queerness since they were fifteen. She'd been to Pride marches, joined the LGBT society at university, watched every season of *The L Word*.

As we settled into life together and navigated our relationship, I started feeling more and more able to explore, express and articulate my sexuality and my gender. Although, I think it's important to point out that the first conversation we had about me being trans, around a year in, went really badly – I couldn't articulate what I wanted, and Abi filled in the gaps with an immediate and dramatic medical transition that scared them.

I think we both suffered from one-dimensional depictions of trans people, often centered around surgery (I only partially blame *The L Word*). I didn't know if I wanted that. I didn't know I could want something else, something more.

My neurodivergence and madness were medicalised – that means that the way I experienced myself, the world, my body was understood through a psychiatric lens. Psychiatry sees symptoms, diagnosis, treatment. Psychiatry puts doctors in charge. To access the things I needed like support workers, therapy, or a bus pass, I had to consent to this, play along, allow the rich complexity of my experience to be written over with disorders and diagnosis.

Transness is medicalised – that means that the ways people experience gender, themselves, their bodies, outside of the binary is understood through a psychiatric lens. Psychiatry sees symptoms, diagnosis, treatment.

Psychiatry puts doctors in charge. If I want to access things, like surgery, hormones or legally changing my assigned sex, I have to consent to this, play along, allow the rich complexity of my experience to be written over with diagnosis and treatment. Given the state of NHS Gender Identity Services I'd have to be in it for the long haul to get any pay off.

I was talking to my (private) therapist recently about changing my name. I wanted something that wasn't so easy for other people to pin a gender on, but I also didn't want to change it from Lilith; I like that name, I like how many trans(fem) people have that name already, I don't want to have to change something I like about myself just because other people gender it a particular way.

I'd settled on Lea (as in sea) as a contraction of sort of Lilith. When she used it for me as they said goodbye, I felt something unsettling. I stared at my computer screen long after the zoom window had closed. Was this joy? Gender euphoria? Did I feel good about something about myself?

I spent so long hating myself that feeling neutral feels like an achievement, something precious that needs to be treated gently, cultivated, nurtured. I spent so long in crisis that things being stable, even if not good, feels like enough.

For years I didn't dare risk that in pursuit of something as fickle, as dangerous, as destablising and impermanent, as joy. But I want more. I want to explore; I want playfulness and experimentation. I want joyfulness, yes, but I also want to make mistakes, feel bad, change my mind, lower the stakes of transition, of wanting things at all. I want better trans healthcare not to be a question of life and death (which it is).

Negotiating the medicalisation of my transness is complicated by the trauma of psychiatric services, which has made every encounter with medical professionals harder; I have to steel myself beforehand, steady myself when I get home.

Right now, Abi and I are exploring options for having a baby. I can only handle navigating one gatekept service, one intensely medicalised process, one invasive encounter with medical professionals at one time. I can only jump through so many hoops. Sometimes I need to keep my feet on the ground.

I remind myself that just because I am not able to pursue a medical transition through the NHS or private healthcare, doesn't mean that there are no resources for me to explore and trans, my body, my gender. Trans people have been crafting their own and each other's transitions since before the NHS was born. The resources for transition aren't just material (like money or hormones) but include things like language.

Similarly, Mad people have been forming community, sharing support and resources, and crafting understandings of ourselves long before the authors of the DSM thought they could name us. I sent a draft of this essay to a friend who challenged me, asking whether it is easier to imagine a transness outside of a medical gaze, suggesting that I'm more comfortable reclaiming my experience as a trans person from medicine than my experience as a mad person.

It certainly feels more fragile. I suspect it's because I've always kept my transness shielded from medicine, whereas my madness was forged in the fires of mental health services.

I grieve the possibilities that weren't open to me because of the ways we medicalise neurodivergence and madness and transness. I feel a deep anger and sadness that I was denied playfulness, exploration, space, freedom, that in shielding my queerness from the problematising gaze of psychiatrists I never got to bring it out into the light and look at it.

Equally, I feel a deep gratitude for the networks, communities, people now and in the past, who have given me the possibilities and resources to play, explore, articulate and express myself, unstable as it is. I feel thankful for every mad and trans zine maker who has shone a light on themselves, no matter how brief, illegible, or badly aligned on a photocopier.

MY SENSE OF SELF, OR YOUR SENSE OF ME?
- Hattie Porter

I was eighteen years old when I first heard the word non-binary. It was the same year the psychiatrist told me I had borderline personality disorder – a diagnosis categorised by unstable and intense emotions, unstable and intense relationships, unstable and intense fears and an unstable and intense sense of self. Or something like that.

I was sent away holding a crumpled leaflet, left with my unanswered questions to figure out if this was an illness or an insult; a question I still haven't found the answer to. What caught my attention most was the words 'unstable sense of self' explained as 'the patient's own self-image, aims and internal preferences are often unclear or disturbed'. I read this over and over again but couldn't understand whether this referred to how I see myself or how others see me. It wasn't the first time I'd been told my self-image was disturbed, although I was more familiar with this language from playground bullies than psychiatrists.

As a non-binary, autistic person there is often a great canyon between the way I see myself and the way other people see me. I exist in a space outside what is deemed possible. Yet my identity is not viewed as proof that these 'impossibilities' are possible; rather it is assessed as some form of sickness. I haven't always called myself non-binary, but I have always lived in the space between the binary boxes which weren't built for me.

For so much of my life I did not have the luxury of a word which made any sense to me. Discovering there is a word which reflects who I am gave me a sense of possibility and freedom to be nothing and everything, to be myself. But I haven't always had that freedom. As a child, the only resources I had to learn about queerness were the heavy words carved into the toilet doors and the language of playground bullying. That's how I learnt being queer was synonymous with being flawed. That's how I learnt to hide this part of me in complex folds of origami, bury it deep inside and seal it with my shame. That's how I learnt to survive. And it came with a price.

***

Transgender and non-binary people are more likely to have mental illness than cisgender people, which is not surprising considering the onslaught of prejudice and discrimination we face. This abuse takes a toll on the community, and transgender people's mental health suffers as a result. Research has also shown transgender people are more likely to have a 'personality disorder', especially borderline personality disorder. That is to say, transgender people are more likely to be *diagnosed* with borderline personality disorder. *Diagnosed* as a verb.

Borderline personality disorder is a highly contested and controversial diagnosis. The diagnosis has faced criticism regarding its conceptual foundations, history and application.

Patients feel this is a diagnosis attached to those who are disliked or considered 'difficult' by psychiatrists, with women making up 75% of those diagnosed with this modern-day equivalent of hysteria or witchcraft.

The diagnosis can be considered as a weapon of social control, designed to silence women who deviate from social norms and dare to fight against the ways they are oppressed.

Borderline personality disorder has long been considered one of the most stigmatised psychiatric diagnoses, with this stigma and judgement seemingly most prominent within medical communities. Without pouring the words out onto the page, I can attest I have certainly felt harmed by this diagnosis and have experienced it being used as justification to deny me basic care, compassion and humanity. My (mis)diagnosis of borderline personality disorder prevented the access to identification and assessment of autism, blocking access to the appropriate support and resources I needed.

It feels to me beyond mere coincidence that transgender people, an extremely stigmatised and marginalised group of people, get lumped with this diagnosis at higher rates than others. Indeed, the history of transgender oppression is heavily entwined with the constructs of personality disorders. Being trans, like being gay, has historically been considered a mental illness and was first described in 1952 as one of the 'sociopathic personality disturbances.'. In 1980, the *DSM-III* (Diagnostic and Statistical Manual of Mental Disorders (*DSM-III*) described transgender people as having coexisting personality disturbances. It also added 'uncertainty of gender identity' as an example of identity disturbance in those with borderline personality disorder. Much of the literature about transgender people published around this time considered being trans a personality disorder in itself.

Transgender identities remain in the International Classification of Diseases (ICD) and DSM diagnostic manuals as 'gender incongruence' and 'gender dysphoria', respectively. It was only in January 2022, when the *ICD-11* (International Classification of Diseases) came into operation that it finally stopped considering being transgender a mental illness. However, this long history of pathologisation remains in the collective consciousness and is often cited by those who firmly disbelieve in the human rights of transgender people. It is part of their reasoning for these views.

This positioning of transgender identities as mental illnesses implicitly says, 'I don't believe you', 'you're wrong', 'you are not really the gender you say you are, you're just ill and disordered'. It's pretty futile attempting to argue with these people who are so cemented in their position. A position which hasn't come from nowhere, but rather has been well supported by the institution of psychiatry through the past century and into the present day.

So psychiatry might not *explicitly* label transgender people as disordered at the very core and integral essence of their person by psychiatry. Yet we many of us are labelled with borderline personality disorder at higher rates than others. Is this implicit pathologisation? Most of the research regarding this stretches in one of two directions, asking either: Are trans people more likely to have 'borderline personality disorder'? Or are those with 'borderline personality disorder' more likely to be trans?

The first question addresses the experiences of stigma and discrimination transgender people face and suggests that as a result of this trauma they may be more likely to develop maladaptive personality traits. It is certainly important to consider the impact of the harms and traumatic experiences trans people face but there is something ironically cruel in sticking a label on people which would attract further stigma and discrimination, when their reactions are entirely proportional to the stigma and prejudice they face.

The second question considers whether people with a borderline personality disorder label are more likely to identify as trans. This suggests that characteristics of the personality disorder such as an unstable sense of self may make someone more likely to think they're trans or turn to questioning their gender as a way to manage underlying instability. For people who do not know what it is like to be trans I really can't stress this enough: I did not just wake up one morning and decide to be trans for a laugh, or because I was bored and unfulfilled. I won't waste my breath arguing.

A third option, which is rarely acknowledged in these studies, is the role of psychiatrist bias in the diagnosis of borderline personality disorder in trans people. There are no robust studies examining this – a serious gap in the research given the prevalence and impact of the diagnosis – but there is significant evidence for the role of bias in diagnosing borderline personality disorder in other minority communities. For example, lesbian, gay and bisexual people have been shown to be more likely to be diagnosed with borderline personality disorder when the psychiatrist is aware of their sexuality. In general, misdiagnosis and medical errors are more likely to occur when the patient is of a more marginalised social status than the psychiatrist.

One of the studies considering borderline personality disorder in transgender people used two methods to assess the rates of personality pathology in the group. Firstly, patients completed a self-reported questionnaire. This was followed by a structured interview with a psychiatrist. Whilst the clinician interview suggested almost 50% of the transgender patient sample met the criteria for having at least one personality disorder, with borderline personality disorder being the most prevalent. The self-report questionnaire revealed something different: these patients had fewer unhealthy personality traits than their cisgender counterparts.

The difference in these results was attributed to patients being guarded in their self-reports and subsequently answering untruthfully. However, the role of bias cannot be ignored here. Are psychiatrists more likely to diagnose a personality disorder in transgender patients? Does this diagnosis continue to serve as a means of social control by silencing those who deviate from what is expected of them in gendered social norms and expectations? I have my own answers to these questions. I hope this chapter encourages you to think about your answers.

I can't go back to comfort my 18-year-old self as they clutched the leaflet with the stinging words 'unstable sense of self'. I can't tell them the things they are yet to learn and the comfort and understanding they will find. But if I could say just one thing, I'd tell my younger self: it's not my sense of self which is unstable, it's the world's sense of me.

Everything they call instability is me learning to unravel the way I was taught to dress in shame and self-hatred. It is me unpicking the stitches of the clothes I never grew into, working out what parts are me, and what parts are the costume I created to protect myself. This is me relearning the language I was taught as a child, and it is hard work. Some days this is messy. Some days everything is a lie. But I am finally learning how to let myself be myself and to love myself for whoever that may be, even if I don't really know yet.

I am proud to be queer, but it is not always easy. People are not always kind. I am always 'other', and this demands that I navigate the process of coming out and 'admitting' to being who I am. This is in itself instability. This is an experience of having to declare to the world that my identity is incongruent with their default assumptions. This is a continuous process of opening yourself up again and again to everyone you meet, allowing yourself to be vulnerable, never sure how you'll be perceived. And that is instability.

'You are a victim of the violence of the boxes that bind you
The boxes that restrict and then confine you,
That try to define you
And I can't fucking breathe in this space
I can't breathe
When my breath is measured
By the shape of the shame in yours'

> YOU ARE A VICTIM OF
> THE VIOLENCE OF THE BOXES
> THAT BIND YOU
> THE BOXES THAT RESTRICT AND
> THEN CONFINE YOU, THAT TRY TO DEFINE YOU
> AND I CAN'T FUCKING BREATHE IN THIS SPACE
> I CAN'T BREATHE
> WHEN MY BREATH IS MEASURED
> BY THE SHAPE OF THE SHAME IN YOURS

Hattie Porter

Embroidery on binder – an item used by trans masculine people to compress and reduce appearance of their chest.

16

THAT'S NOT MY NAME…. Jo Doll

1.

The cheap white stickers are laid out on the table again, each one featuring the name of a group member written in bland black marker.

It is the third week of a 12-week long programme, the third time I have walked into this cold featureless room and the third time my makeshift name badge has been wrong.

The name I was bestowed at birth is staring up at me mockingly from the Formica surface, waiting to be placed on my top at the insistence of the facilitator. I grab the flimsy paper and sit in my assigned seat, frustrated.

People drift into the session. Pleasantries are exchanged and the group settles in for the next instalment of Emotion Focus. There are introductions, some reflections from the last meeting and other things said though I couldn't tell you what as my mind is whirring with the silent barrage of my inner monologue.

The name I was handed at birth stands as a painful reminder of a past endured.

It is an instant gender marker, chosen to define my existence along with a set of rules and biases laid out for those who read or hear it to associate with me, a person they have never met.

Every time I send or receive an email within the organisation, it's there. Every time I meet a new member of psychological services in the revolving door of my treatment, it is there.

I have raised the mistake before, politely explaining for the 179452nd time that this is not what I am called, how it is important to me that my gender-neutral abbreviation is recognised. I clearly asked to have my choices respected at both the pre-group assessment and first session introduction segment. This was met with confused nodding and patronising concern but ultimately ignored and has most certainly been forgotten by the time my notes are written up.

Somehow, I make it through to the break. We are invited to go outside or use the comfort facilities, and all at once I am simmering with a white-hot sensation. I need to get out of here - now.

I become aware that I am walking, striding even away from the building... fingers clamped around my phone... heart pounding in my ears.

The uphill battle to be heard starts and ends with my identity. As with many others lost in the mental health system, my choices are cast aside by the avalanche of paperwork the NHS insists on using to define us.

I have a sizeable list of troubling examples that involve different departments and Trusts. The last decade of being a mental health service user has been as problematic as the trauma that led me to utilise the system in the first place. Too ill for certain pathways, not ill enough for others, I have been parked in the admin system for years, all the while being prescribed more and more medication even though I have regularly expressed a desire to reduce my chemical reliance.

The pills keep me safe, and safe equals OK to the NHS. Not living or thriving or being happy - just not wanting to die.

I have volunteered hundreds of hours to mental health services, both NHS and third party. They consult me when the Trust wants to showcase how proactive they are in co-production or how inclusive they are...add some other bandwagon metrics here... And yet the same Trust does not recognise my preferred name or pronouns

The data says I am in the tick-box pile that proves the Trust are performing acceptably. They send letters occasionally, and I don't want to kill myself – so ding, ding, ding! Good job, everyone, we earnt our 50k salary today!

2.

I am not a fan of labels but in this instance they may be the clearest way to introduce myself on the page. I am an AFAB person that identifies as non-binary. I prefer they/them but understand that the majority of people I come into contact with will assume my gender/pronouns based on my physical appearance. I do not have any desire to have transformative surgery, and I do not associate these attributes with my sexuality. I suppose the easiest descriptor would be queer pansexual.

I was raised in a religious household, taught not to ask questions and led to believe that emotion was bad and subservience was good. Growing up, the females around me were dependent, dramatic and martyrish characters, intent on career motherhood and only invested in the latest scandal in Albert Square.

Intelligence and ambition were pursuits of the male, and as a female, I was to concern myself with being attractive and attentive in order to 'bag a husband' and fulfil my ultimate role as a child bearer.

This never felt right to me. Ever.

I didn't like Barbie or dressing up. I didn't get into make-up when my peers did and I hated having long hair. I found respite at my Grandad's house, the place I could be myself. Playing in the small flowerbed he had said was just for me, digging up worms and having dirt under my nails was bliss. I would spend hours building structures out of the ancient Meccano set abandoned by one of my uncles in years past, lying on the floor in quiet concentration, tiny spanner in hand.

As a teenager, I had to keep my teachers happy by doing well and my family happy by not doing too well. The shadow of the other me had begun to cast itself over my everyday life.

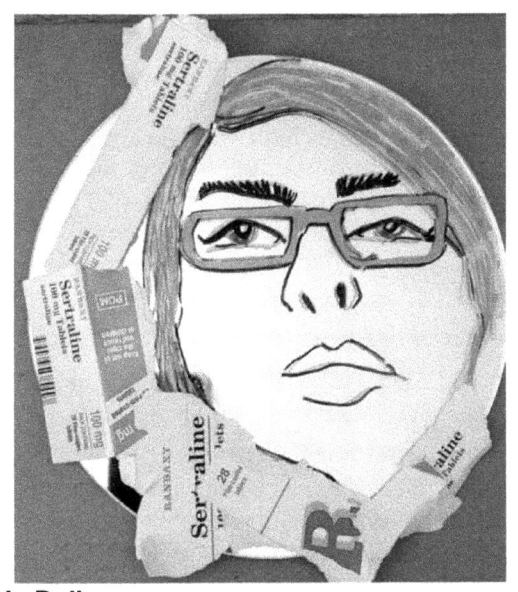

Jo Doll

3.

I was subjected to several traumatic events over the course of my early adulthood. My choices over my own body and mind were taken away. They were stolen both by individuals - some of whom were family - and the formal bodies charged with my care.

When a consultant I saw told me I wouldn't have children, I had no visible reaction. I was never offered counselling or a follow-up appointment. I was 19.

When my front door was smashed down by a team of police to arrest my then partner, I had no visible reaction. I was never offered any support or counselling. I lost my everything that day. I lost myself.

The reason for this explanation is not for sympathy or point scoring (yes, some people do keep a tally when you open up about mental health). It is for context: to demonstrate that I am able to be open and articulate about my struggles.

This ability to convey insight is not the key to support people may imagine it to be. When I speak this candidly, it is interpreted as inspirational, strong and even cured. But where others see insight, I see the burden of knowledge.

4.

As I type this, it has been 12 years, 7 months and 1 week since my breakdown.

My clinical labels are Borderline Personality Disorder (BPD), Generalised Anxiety Disorder (GAD) and Complex Trauma (C-PTSD). And while my gender identity hasn't been reflected in my notes (more on that later!), the NHS would record that as Gender Dysphoria, formerly known as Gender Identity Disorder (GID). I detest these terms, each one a convenient shorthand for hidden preconceptions and traits used solely to abbreviate a life.

Much of my experience with mental health services has been negative – from the insistence on using jargon and acronyms to the damaging linear treatment pathways. While each department, team and Trust may implement their own slight variation, the fact remains that the NHS is a business first.

I am not about to dive into the sociopolitical nuances of how and why this is the case. Most service users don't care how the machine works; they just want to buy the cure.
In many medical disciplines, this is an acceptable, maybe even preferable way to approach patient ailments - but mental health is anything but simple. The cruel irony for most seeking support for this type of illness is that despite constantly promoting talk therapy, the system actively parks vulnerable people on waiting lists. Very often these exceed two years.

In my own meandering path to gaining an understanding of the trauma responses I am plagued by this state of limbo has been debilitating. The initial relief I felt when I asked my GP for help was almost instantly replaced by anxiety at the now familiar indifference of a system where there is always another administrative faux pas or procedural change that results in more time waiting.

More hours, days and weeks of fatigue and feeling uncomfortable in my own skin.

5.

My gender and sexuality have been a recurring cause of anxiety for me. In an attempt to reduce the judgements, I hid that facet of myself for a long turbulent time.

This came up in a one-to-one session during my first stint of psychological services.

The weekly hour-long meetings were meant to address my diminishing emotional tolerance. As such, my childhood was a subject that my therapist chose to delve into repeatedly like an excited puppy in autumn leaves.

My upbringing left a lot to be desired. My family were (and still are) very narrow in their thinking about most things. Many of my interests were either ridiculed or dismissed, my intelligence seen as some kind of barrier by my parents. Fast forward to a few decades later, and I am sitting in this drab counselling room wading through the torrent of confusion I call a mind.

We're talking about my extremes again.

The large sheet of cheap copier paper is now covered in notes, all written by them, and being pushed towards me.

In black ink the words 'little girl' and 'bitch' sit at either end of a hastily drawn line.

'...so how do we find balance, Joanne?'

I wince inwardly at being called by that name. I am not, nor have I ever felt like a Joanne.

I don't remember exactly how the topic of sexuality came up during the session. What I do remember is the weight of the gaze I felt as the words left my mouth. I opened up, as I had been encouraged to do - and immediately regretted being so candid. In that moment, everything and nothing changed, the sound of judgement being passed upon my choices was deafening, almost rivaling the silence in the room.

'Is it possible that you indulge in this lifestyle to please your partner? That you (as a woman) are having your vulnerability exploited, manipulated to fulfil their own desires...?'

The question, which sounded more like a statement, stung like ice cold water on unsuspecting skin. Hurtful? Callous? Misinformed? Stereotypical? I can't decide which is the most appropriate word - I just know that my trust shattered, and inside I was screaming 'SEE? This is why WE HIDE WHO WE ARE! How are you still this NAIVE!!!!?'

The casual tone somehow made the words sting more. It wasn't quite pity but nor was it disdain. The thinly veiled implication that I could not possibly enjoy sex unless coerced felt particularly insulting, more than being misgendered (again) and more than the doubt cast over the strength of my relationship.

I explained that I had spent a long time exploring and questioning my sexuality and the ramifications of my past trauma upon these feelings. I elaborated on the
understanding that my partner and I have in this regard, that we revisit our 'rules' regularly and always discuss the possible outcome for our relationship. All the time I sat there talking, I felt like I was justifying my sexuality and defending my choice to reclaim my own pleasure.

I left that session shell-shocked. The lingering air of judgment clung to me like smoke from a bonfire in early winter, only not as easy to remove.

Mental health is complicated. It doesn't follow a pattern or have a specific rule set. The medical model insists on dissecting people into separate pieces, each inspected and adjudicated by professional teams that work in parallel rather than conjunction.

My identity is directly impacted by my mental health, which seems too obvious to say but is lost on the majority of health care services.

I am not a problem to be fixed. My identity is not a symptom of illness. My behaviour does not need correcting - yet every aspect of my psychological services experience has been underlined by the term 'disorder'. Sexuality is not a disorder. Identity does not need explanation.

How hard is it to see me as a person that has been through hell at the hands of others? Why does who I choose to allow in my bed have any place in my medical notes? To what end? For whose eyes? I don't need a 56-page handbook and monthly supervision meetings to know how to interact with those who have different lifestyles to mine. I know how to be a respectful, kind human being - isn't that supposed to be the cornerstone of the caring profession…?

JO DOLL

THERE ARE SCRATCHY WOOLLEN JUMPERS UNDER MY SKIN – Z Mennell

1.

I should try to start when this starts, but it doesn't even start with me. It started somewhere way back and has mutated with each generation, distilled into the amalgam of defects and disorders that make up my NHS psychiatric file. I have had so many middle-aged straight male psychiatrists fixate on my mother; they are barely interested in my absent fathers, biological *and* ideological. They would ask in the first twenty minutes, 'how was your birth?', the theory being that if it was difficult, then that must be the root of my disordered upbringing and childhood. I'm told plenty of studies back this up, and I could research them here, but what would that do?

So here I'll say, yes, my birth was difficult. My mum had been sent home from the hospital – I was setting up my lifelong habit of arriving late – it was 1994, and I was her fourth child. She was alone when I came out covered in a fleshy bag like a newborn lamb. Tearing it open, she saw that the umbilical cord was wrapped twice around my neck. I assume she untangled me. Little me wasn't breathing; my mum put her fingers in my mouth and pulled out the mucus and shit that had clogged my airways. I had ingested and breathed in my own shit. The flap of skin intended to keep the twice-digested food safely inside my colon whilst inside my amniotic sac and during birth had broken due to the stress on my body. I write this knowing everything that follows. I write this knowing that I took a breath some time after. I don't know if I cried then, but I am crying now.

It is mid-November 2017. I am in a room with a cream floor flecked in faux terrazzo- style lino that goes halfway up the walls. There is a small bedside table, a larger chest of drawers, a window that does not open, mottled orange curtains, white walls that curve indistinguishably into the same colour ceiling. A single bed is in the centre of the room with pastel yellow and white sheets and one thin pillow. The door is narrow and tall and has a small circular window five-and-a-half feet up with frosted glass in lines. There is a lock on the door, but I cannot lock or unlock it. It will be two more years before I learn that every fixture in this room has been designed to break under the weight of a human body.

I am sitting on the bed. The door has been locked for the night, but my lights are still on; lights are allowed on until 11pm. 'You must be in your room by 10pm at the latest, no exceptions.' I sit on the crinkling plastic mattress and masturbate furiously. It is the only thing I can do to dissipate the ferocious waves crashing against the inside of my skin and swirling about my ankles, filling my toes. From the confusing mess of items in my bag, they have taken my drugs, pens and pencils, metal ruler, all liquids and toiletries, even the Bonjela for my incessant mouth ulcers, but they haven't taken my belt. Maybe out of pity as I have been wearing the same clothes for four days, and these trousers hardly stay up without one. Maybe they just didn't see it since it was covered by my baggy shirt.

The bed creaks, so I freeze, waiting to hear if anyone is approaching my door to slide apart the frosted bands in the glass and peek in at me. Nothing happens, so I continue, one hand on my dick and the other wrapped in the black leather band and pulling, the metal buckle pinching at the thin skin on the front of my neck.

I feel my whole head turn red and the water inside it Mediterranean warm, lapping gently at the edges of my ears. As though my head is submerged in a hot candlelit bath while the rest of me is in a drafty fluorescent room. I can taste piss in the air, whether it's from the curtains or the bed I don't know. It could be in the walls or the foundations for all I know, years of stagnant piss pooling underneath the floors. I huff it in, sweet and tangy on my tongue. Maybe this is what people taste when they talk about posh white wine? I finish, but the belt doesn't loosen. One hand stops, and the other continues steadfast, the leather creaking against itself. As the room disappears slowly in a blossoming of petrol-coloured blotches, my hand goes slack, and air rushes through me, churning the water into a fevered storm again. The lights go off. I wipe myself on the sheets and, at some point, fall asleep, a bitter urine taste like stale black tea hitting the back of my throat.

2.

It is 2019, and I am in a WeWork interior designers wet-dream of a meeting room – all complementing, low pile patches of mustard and grey carpet on the walls and floor, and leather lounge chairs nestled in glass walls. After Essex NHS trust failed to follow up with my medication reviews, I have not taken any medication for almost two years. I moved from Essex to Hackney and then lived in Balham for a few months; for the past three years, I have not lived in any one place for longer than four months. As my mental health deteriorated, I was forced to interrupt my university studies for two years.

Now I'm back trying to study but am still waiting for support from the NHS, so my university has offered this appointment with their private psychiatrist.

He is sitting opposite me in this small room, looking only at the screen of his MacBook on his lap. He is cold and distant. He asks me about my mother, my birth and my diagnosis. He asks why I feel like I need help. He asks me about my sexuality, my gender, my sex life. When I tell him I am gay, he touches his chin. I tell him that I identify as a man; he says 'good'. I tell him candidly that I have a reasonable amount of casual sex and that, yes, I engage in fetish sexual activities.

He tells me that I am engaging in risky, self-destructive behaviour, and my sex life is equivalent to taking hard drugs. This straight man who has only just met me tells me I should curb my sexual activities and improve myself – I should stop being so self-indulgent and lazy. He prescribes me a sedative occasionally used as a mood stabiliser; he tells me it is mild and I will have no side effects. I take the medication twice a day for 18 months. During this time, I am in a permanent haze: I oversleep, I stumble and slur my words regularly and I accidentally cut and burn myself when cooking in the kitchen.

I never have a review or follow-up appointment with him. I email three times and get no reply. When Southwark takes over my care, I am told that carbamazepine is not a light and easygoing medication and that it is quite a strong sedative. It takes two months to bring the dosage down weekly to nothing.

3.

Holding the past *and* the present and the hazy possibility of the future at the same time, my mind dredges up a moment from before the locked room and leather belt.

It is 2016; I have spent two years at university struggling with work and life. On-campus my GP looks me up and down repeatedly as she asks me ten simple questions. She tells me it's probably not that I'm *autistic*, but it could be *ADHD*. I feel the pins and needles of a new sensation about how the world relates to me, the first stings of the clinical glance that only a healthcare professional can give.

This is passed onto the university, who pay for me to have a specific learning differences assessment. Over four hours I face a barrage of seemingly unrelated tests about how shapes fit together, how I hold a pen, how I walk and how I structure sentences. The education specialist tells me that my profile is very spiky and that I am *dyspraxic* and *dyslexic*. The word 'vindication' flashes in my mind as relief circulates around my body knowing that my struggle isn't a moral failing of my character. These conditions 'exist on a continuum.' She tells me she cannot diagnose ADHD but strongly recommends I pursue this diagnosis on the NHS.

4.

I wait a year for my first appointment with the Autism & ADHD specialist in Harrow. When we meet, I haven't slept for three days.

I have been taking my medication, as prescribed by a psychiatrist I saw in Homerton Hospital four months earlier. It has taken over two months for the summary letter and prescription to be released to my GP. It's for an anti-depressant called venlafaxine.

A week before the ADHD appointment, I have an electrocardiogram in preparation. Measuring the electrical activity in my heart is a delicate process; if I breathe too fast, it impacts the accuracy, as do the pneumatic drills outside and my mobile phone in my pocket. I sweat profusely, so the pads won't stay put.

After several printouts and packets of sticky electrode pads, they give me the clearest results they can get and refer me to a heart specialist.

In the ADHD specialist's office, she tells me she cannot assess me as I am displaying signs that I am in crisis. I agree. I talk at her for an hour. In desperation I tell her every detail and tangent detected by my erratic and splintered consciousness. She tells me to go to A&E. I go home and go to bed.

The following day I go to my GP, who has received a letter from the specialist detailing her assessment of my need for immediate crisis care. My GP tells me to go home and wait to hear from them.

I spend a week at home eating pancakes and drinking dessert wine every day. 'You deserve nice things; you're struggling,' I tell myself. I hear from no one, so I call my GP, who tells me to call Chelsea and Westminster. They ask me to call Newham as I live in their area. A person on the phone at Newham asks me what's wrong. In response, I ramble and rant the whole story, sparing no detail. They say they don't understand; what do I want from them?

I ask for help. They tell me to wait; I wait a week and hear nothing.

I am still taking venlafaxine as prescribed.

Finally, my job says that it is unsafe for me to work, so I stay home. I cancel my trip to Hong Kong, expecting that some support will come and I will be taken to hospital. My GP tells me to keep taking my medication. The ADHD specialist tells me to wean myself off it slowly. Chelsea & Westminster say to stick to my current care plan and take all medication as prescribed. Newham tells me they don't know and that I am not under their care.

I am on the Qatar Airways flight from Heathrow. My ticket says Monday 30th October 2017. I am going to Hong Kong for a week.

5.

When I come back to London, I don't remember anything. I sift through the hundreds of photos I took and feel a distance from myself. My vision is filled with the grainy noise of a bad photograph; my ears are plugged with static from an old TV. A week later, having stopped taking the venlafaxine sometime in the past fortnight, I go to see my personal tutor at university. After thirty minutes, she tells me that she can't let me leave on my own.

She goes to call an ambulance to collect me. I promise her that I will walk across the Thames westward to St Thomas' A&E. I do just that.

6.

Fast forward to four years later.

I am sitting upright in front of my laptop, and the small white light flashes next to the camera above the screen. It captures me sitting at my desk and broadcasting it to another computer in the office of a small pale woman with deep red hair. Her camera seems to loom over her. I do not know how tall she is.

She speaks with a bright Irish accent.

  'It's the gold standard'.

She's talking about the new therapy pathway I'm being offered. A year ago, I was referred to the community mental health services in Southwark, having just moved there from nearby Lewisham. My new GP took one look at my NHS notes (the few that he could access) and realised something wasn't right.

After a two-hour phone call, he had a better picture. He listened to me talk about my experiences and assured me that he would do everything he could to get me some sort of mental health support in place. After a few months of waiting, I was seen by this young psychiatrist on placement. She spent six weeks meeting with me on Microsoft Teams, asking a raft of questions I'd been asked countless times before. She wanted insight, she said, into my mental health history and, more importantly, my perspective and feelings.

This is the last of these sessions. The red-haired woman has spent 45 minutes reading through the report she has written for me and about me, taking account of everything I said. Nothing seemed to be *that* altered. This is a first. With 15 minutes to go, she tells me that they think my diagnosis needs to be changed from *bipolar* to *EUPD*.

I sigh, daunted and confused. I've lived four years with a diagnosis of bipolar. I know what it is. I know other people who have it. I have read books and seen TV shows where characters have it. It is graspable. I've been taking sedatives on and off. I am tired a lot but sometimes I am not tired at all. This all fits the profile of what I've been told bipolar is. My astrological and Myers Briggs personality type say I have bipolar!

But now this psychiatrist says I have EUPD. I think of Winona Ryder. I saw *Girl, Interrupted* when I was far too young on late-night Film4 via scratchy Freeview. I remember how her difficult, messy, illogical character had borderline personality disorder.

7.

And now it is 2017. I am in Basildon Hospital Mental Health Assessment Unit:

In my stiff hospital socks, I shuffle out of a meeting room where I've just spent 90 minutes crouched on a chair with my lips pushed into the tops of my knees. Opposite me were a team of psychiatrists, doctors, nurses, and carers. They verbally prodded me about school, drugs, university, my thoughts, employment, my feelings, my mother.

'Looks like bipolar, possibly emotionally unstable….' I overhear the leading male psychiatrist say to the other male doctor as the nurse escorts me from the room. Of course, I'm emotionally unstable; who wouldn't be in my situation?!

I walk across the hall into the dayroom, flanked on one side by the kitchen and the other by the quiet room (which is never quiet). My week-old gang of mad friends are there, looking at me expectantly.

'So what did you get?!' one says.

I tell them.

'Oh, they tell all of us we have EUPD. That's borderline, they're obsessed with diagnosing it.'

This lightens the fogginess of what it actually means for me. Our posse leader tells me a few of them had been diagnosed with bipolar. It all feels a little easier to comprehend coming from them, being spoken to like I'm a real person. Someone hands me a packet of crisps, and we all sit down, Jeremy Kyle blaring from the TV inside the Perspex box on the wall.

8.

On Microsoft Teams, my red-headed psychiatrist explains the treatment differences between EUPD and bipolar. She says that because I've had little to no improvement on the mood stabilisers, I might benefit better from the treatment pathways for EUPD. It is July 2021, and she tells me bipolar is usually managed using drugs and not therapy.

I have spent four years waiting to access talking therapies and being told that low-level easy-access cognitive behavioural therapy cannot handle my 'severe' mental illness. I've been told countless times that I shouldn't be working, so my GP has signed me off work. I've been told that I should be in therapy though the CMHT turns down every referral. I've been told that my recently diagnosed ADHD needs to be brought in-line to access proper services. And I have been told to wait three years for ADHD services. After two years of waiting, I have found out I was never placed on the list. I've been told there are no other mental health support structures that I can access.

A memory arises from June 2020. I have been evicted from my house. Signed off work and unemployed for the past seven months, I find whatever room I can afford on my pitifully low universal credit. This happens to be two miles away, just within the borders of the neighbouring NHS trust.

9.

There is a date I remember.

25th November 2017.

The day I was released from the hospital.

Four weeks and two days later, I am watching TV at home alone, drowsy from my sedatives. I am awake at least.

The crisis support nurse has just had her daily visit, during which she asked how suicidal I am. She made notes about my eye contact; told me to do 'as much work as possible and that 'the drowsiness will pass.' I am watching the news that Carrie Fisher has just died. The presenters talk at length about how she lived her life with manic depression in the public eye. She battled and died from her addictions. My head is lolling about as I gaze up at the screen, and I weep for a celebrity I find myself suddenly connected to and now severed from.

Only writing this chapter, I find out that she died at the end of 2016. And so I slide out of the open window as the world goes sideways. Falling into the sky, I realise that linear time doesn't exist. These are more than memories bouncing off of each other. They break and meld together. They change me and my world the same way the webcam light changes my posture.

meets the diagnostic criteria

a history of dysregulation of his mood,

He also presents with considerable risk

ZMennell – Birdsong Collage 1

ZMennell – Birdsong Collage 2

ZMennell – Birdsong Collage 3

THE MENTAL HEALTH SYSTEM IS HERE TO POLICE YOUR GENDER

18

CLOSETS AND REVELATIONS: A MADLESQUE VARIETY SHOW – Cal (pen name)

Catherine D'lish, icon of the neoburlesque, has advice for those wishing to perfect the art of fan dancing. Burlesque hopefuls must 'work on it up until their hands feel like hamburger meat, then rest and recuperate, and then repeat this sequence until they have become one with their fans.'

As a transgender/non-binary/polyamorous/pansexual trying to survive UK mental health services, this process sounds sort of familiar. Admittedly not the ethereal grace of the fans, or the sparkling costumes. There have never been adoring audiences. Despite this, I have become skilled in my own far less sexy version of the dance. As I move through consultations, assessments and therapies, I practise covering, revealing, shifting position, covering again, censoring and exposing until I feel like hamburger meat. Every interaction is curated and censored in an attempt to get the treatment I need. Any slip-ups and I risk ruining my performance of the deserving patient, and my true sexuality, gender and lifestyle are pathologised and noted down as Problems To Be Addressed.

After 12 years, I have finally received a diagnosis of CPTSD. Throughout those long and lonely years, I often wondered if the experts were right (they do have lots of letters after their names after all) and the real problem was all this gay-ness?

My deep mistrust of mental health professionals started early in my Madlesque career:

At 16, I sat on the living room couch, looking across at the CAMHS nurse seated opposite. How he expected to have an open conversation with me whilst my parents were in the very next room I don't know. Perhaps if I had lived in a city I could have attended a clinic, with patient rooms and background music to stop eavesdropping. As it was, I felt I was in some sort of peep show. Anything I revealed could be glimpsed by voyeurs at the doors and windows.

> *This nurse gives me a knowing smile.*
> *'Why do you dress like that?' he asks.*
> *I knew what he means, but I also don't understand the question. My confusion must be obvious. He asks again.*
> *'Why do you dress like that, like, differently to others? So you stand out?'*
> *I look at him again. This isn't the direction I expected the conversation to go in. Why aren't we talking about my anorexia, or the self-harm, or the suicidal ideation?*
> *'I don't know,' I answer. 'I just like dressing this way.'*
>
> *He recommends that I wear 'normal' clothes to college this week and 'see how it goes'.*
>
> *And because he is a professional, and the only person offering me a path out of my situation, I try. I try every day. Each time fear grips me as I approach the door, and the clawing discomfort always finds me changing clothes last minute.*
>
> *At our next appointment, I explain what had happened. He smiles, knowingly.*

'Ah, I see,' he says. 'You're a procrastinator.'

***

Once I had escaped the family home and found a queer community to live in, I became more confident disclosing my sexuality. Despite this, I still encountered professionals who were reluctant to accept any deviation from heterosexuality. I would mention I was dating a woman, and they would reply: 'Maybe you're just a straight woman who dates other women?' I would mention the LGBTQIA+ community I had found a home in. They'd respond: 'Perhaps it's these new friends that are influencing your behaviour, hmm?'

However much I tried to open my feather fans and reveal myself to the world, the professionals were determined to cover me up again. After a point, I decided it wasn't worth mentioning my girlfriend at all, let alone telling them I sometimes date *multiple* women! That would have been career suicide. Many Madlesque performers know the risks of honesty in a clinical environment. Explain that you're polyamorous and it is immediately noted down as proof of illness. I am told that having multiple partners proves you have attachment issues. Perhaps it does, but I'm not sure being monogamous proves that you don't.

It wasn't just the queer joy in my life that was being erased. The very real threat of homophobic violence seemed also seemed to be unrecognised.

I'm attending a zoom appointment, and the trauma nurse I'm meeting is kind, and encouraging. She's the first person to identify that my mental health issues are trauma-based. She explains many aspects of my life that I have been battling for years without understanding why.

We're discussing my fear of leaving my flat. She asks me what I am afraid might happen if I left the safety of my home.

> 'Someone might yell at me, and try to intimidate me.'
> She looks concerned.
> 'Has that ever happened?' she asks.
> I look at her. 'Well, yes. Especially when I was walking with my girlfriend.'
> She looks surprised.
> 'People really shouted at you? And yelled abuse? Because they saw two women holding hands? That's awful.'
> I sit silently, waiting to move on from the topic.

How do I explain to this trauma professional that homophobia exists? Maybe she has never had queer patients before. More likely, she's had queer patients but none of them felt safe enough to tell her about their sexuality. Is that worse? I don't know.

***

Over the years I've made a lot of calls to out-of-hour crisis numbers, usually in the early hours of the morning when living inside my own mind has become unbearable. I am aware that the training for this highly skilled work is variable. Some people I spoke to on those seemingly endless nights have been great and helped get me through until morning. Some have been … less so. One phone operator seemed to firmly believe that everyone's goal was to marry someone of a different gender and procreate. He felt the most important thing to tell me, in my moment of crisis, was that one day I too could achieve this highly desirable lifestyle.

He said: 'That's what I want for you' as I tried to explain that finding a boyfriend was not the issue. He said: 'Well, I still have hope that you could have this' as I explained my current focus was not on marriage but on getting through the night. I didn't bother mentioning that even if I did have a child, I wouldn't be able to write my true gender on the birth certificate. There was no point in explaining that non-binary gender identities are not officially recognised; that legally the 'me' I know to be me does not, in fact, exist; that the law is talking over my shoulder to the ghost behind me.

Many professionals have seemed to believe that dating a boy would solve my problems. Looking back, I can say with confidence that this is not the case. I currently date three men, and as lovely as they are, they have not made me any less crazy. Boyfriends cannot replace adequate and accessible healthcare. No relationship can. The belief that meeting Mr. Right would solve all a young girl's problems is one I encountered regularly in teenage fiction and rom coms, but it should not have any place in mental health treatment. As I have aged, things have changed a little. In the past when I reached out to mental health services, they asked if I had a boyfriend. Now they ask if I have a cat. Is this progress?

***

At one point in my life, I (accidentally) did a convincing performance of a straight cisgender woman. Even then, it didn't seem like my wellbeing was considered important to the plan. It shouldn't have surprised me that if you remove transphobia and homophobia from the equation, misogyny is still alive and well.

It was coming to the end of my 5-minute GP appointment. I was embarrassed to ask the question, but I had been building up to asking and I knew if I didn't ask now I never would. We had discussed the change in medications, the treatment options open to me, the waiting lists I could join. No need to be embarrassed, I thought, doctors must talk about this sort of thing all the time. I took a deep breath.

'These meds I'm on,' I started, gripping the sides of my chair. 'Well, my sex drive seems to have completely disappeared.'
The doctor looked at me. He shrugged.
'Yes?' he said.

I lost all the courage I had been gathering, and made a hasty U-turn.

'Oh, nothing,' I replied, lowering my gaze and picking up my bag to leave.

As I walked out of the office, I scolded myself. I should have known that someone as mad as me wasn't meant to have access to a sex life, even if they wanted one. In this setting, the performance was strictly for the pleasure of the audience, not the other way around. I told myself I shouldn't keep kicking up a fuss and getting ill. I should be grateful I even got seen at all. *The GP is a very busy man.*

***

Given my experiences, it is unsurprising that I have never been out as pansexual to a mental healthcare professional. They either assume I'm a straight woman, or they learn that I'm dating women and assume I'm gay. Gay is easier to explain than pansexual.

Well, I mean, pansexuality isn't hard to explain. It's not difficult to understand. But in the world of mental health assessments and treatment, my inability to choose whether I prefer girls or boys could cause all sorts of fireworks. So I stick to one story at a time. God forbid they ever find out I can't decide if I'm a girl or a boy.

And that brings us to gender. It isn't news that Trans folk struggle to access the vital mental healthcare they need. No revelation there. There is a certain irony, then, that the huge waiting times for gender clinics are often justified as a safety precaution against people doing things that would be bad for their ongoing (mental) health.

'We wouldn't want you to make a mistake!' they say.
'Think of the repercussions!'
'Imagine how miserable you would be living in the wrong gender for the rest of your life!'
'Think how hard it would be to get a job!"

Yes, well. Many of us have dealt with that and more. To access trans healthcare in the UK, you have to be diagnosed with a disorder. 'Gender Dysphoria' is the term currently used to pathologise anyone questioning their gender. And helpfully, a GP is given the power to decide whether you have it or not. A detailed assessment takes place (eventually) and at that point you may be told you don't have gender dysphoria after all, and so you don't need the healthcare you have been waiting on. Isn't that a relief!

I spend a lot of time being furious at the current healthcare system. Don't get me wrong, I love the NHS. The last thing I want to see is the sort of privatised healthcare system currently terrorising the United States. But when it comes to trans healthcare, the current NHS provision is totally inadequate.

'Why are the lists so long?' I ask, 'Why do you need a medical diagnosis to have access to trans healthcare? Being trans is not an illness!"

'Well, I mean, you have to check' says the sexual health specialist.

'Check?'

'Check they aren't psychotic. Someone could be psychotic, you know, and think they are a woman even when they're clearly a man.'

I think of my (cisgender) friends who have psychosis and are desperate for adequate healthcare. Surely if the real concern here was for people with psychosis, those friends would be well looked after. Then I think of my friends, current and passed, who have lived for years on waiting lists. I think of the suicides of people who have given up hope of ever accessing the treatment they need, and aren't prepared to live in this state of dysphoria-drenched suspended-animation any longer. They deserved so much better. We deserve so much better.

I keep my Madlesque skills sharp not just for medical appointments but for any dreaded interaction with the DWP. Those of us who rely on disability benefits to survive know all too well the one-on-one performance required to access them.

When I attend my yearly assessment, the fans must work extra hard for an unknown professional, who watches and takes notes and decides if I really am still mad.

Should I mention I'm trans? Will they use that to invalidate my claim? If I mention I have more than one partner, or that I have a partner at all, will they use that to prove I'm a fraud? Can I mention the recent improvements in my mental health? Or should I say nothing has changed? Or should I only mention the things that have got worse? If I say nothing has changed, will they think I'm lying? Will they take away the services I'm accessing? Will they use my performance against me? By this time the fans are drenched in sweat, being whipped back and forth at a giddy speed whilst the assessor calmly asks why I haven't killed myself yet.

***

So, were the experts right? Was the real problem all this gay-ness?

Dearest reader, I don't believe it was.

One day I would love the opportunity to learn a real fan dance, up on a stage that glitters beneath bright lights. If that performance ever happens, I will be doing it all for me. For the thrill of holding an audience captive, in choosing when to tease and when to shock. For rejoicing in my own self, dripping in glamour and sweat and unabashed queer joy.

But for now? I hope for a future where my dance with the mental health services loses its debilitating power dynamic. Maybe one day we could start to choreograph some steps toward wellness and quality of life.

But until that day I will never stop reminding myself that my gayness was never the problem. If this is a dance, I must never forget how skilled us Madlesque performers are, or how many hours of training and blood and sweat and tears it has taken for us to get here. Survival is labour (and not always a labour of love) and that work should be recognised. If I must keep performing, I do it for me, and not for you. If I must keep dancing, I damn well want to get paid for it.

CAL - Anxiety

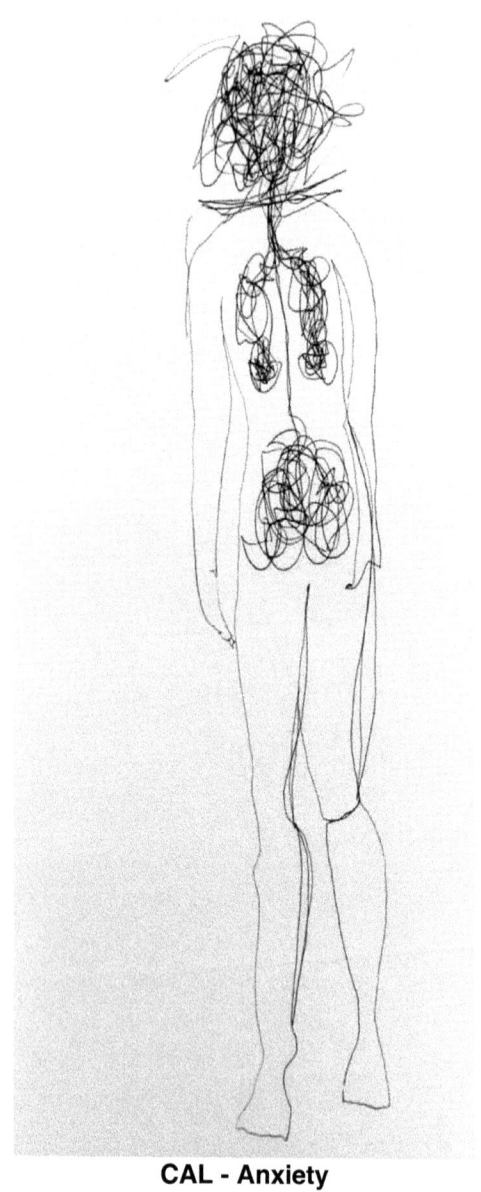

Cal - Welcome Here

19

'WE'RE USED TO IT' – Katie Morison

There is a strange expectation placed on transgender people. When seeking treatment, you can end up being asked a plethora of questions entirely unrelated to the problem at hand. Why? Because staff simply haven't been trained in the matter.

Having been openly transgender for a little over 6 years at the time of writing, I'd like to say I've become used to this. I've become an advocate for my own existence, effectively trained by repeated exposure. This is typical for us in mental health services. Whilst seeking help for anxiety, your conversation is derailed by discussions of 'how you knew' or whatever other questions are on staff members' minds. Whilst some questions can be seen as standard data collection, others are clearly standard curiosity.

Due to this phenomenon alone, often repeated like clockwork, it can take much longer to access basic mental healthcare. What should have been a one-visit problem suddenly becomes two – with NHS wait times measuring this difference in weeks or months. Still, for myself and many others like me, this is the expectation.

For whatever reason, most people believe they will never meet anyone transgender. This leads to the idea that training staff in basic understanding is pointless, and as such, it falls to us to provide on-the-job training on the topic.

The trouble with untrained therapists

I'm very lucky to say that I have access to a therapist, and quite frankly I owe them my life. That said, working with the same person long-term is a sure-fire way to see the lack of training go from simple time-wasting to potentially harmful. I'd been seeing them for over a year by the time this occurred, with the groundwork explanation all done in the months prior.

At the height of one of my depressive periods, the pair of us were discussing where my suicidal urges came from. My depression can be traced to my very early life, including a suicide attempt by age 6. As part of our discussion, my therapist raised a point.
 'In a way, didn't you succeed in killing yourself?'
I paused, then asked for clarification. They suggested that by my choice to transition, the person I used to be was killed. They expressed sympathy for 'the dead', and the session continued on other topics. During the session, I didn't properly process what was said to me. Still, the thought wouldn't leave my head for a few days.

Finally, when I found time to think about it, I worked out why it bothered me so much. The suggestion of guilt. By this logic, someone else would be alive if not for my actions. How selfish I must have been, surely, to allow someone else to die? This was never what the therapist intended, of course – and they would go on to apologise once I brought this up to them.

Once again, I had to advocate for my right to be. In fact, before I transitioned, I'd been dead to the world. I had barely left my room, hated everything about myself and lacked a real identity. The better, and unfortunately less prevalent point of view, is that I was an incomplete work.

By recognising my identity and moving to complete myself, I was finally able to function. We wouldn't say that repairing an object is destroying the broken version, would we?

But we're used to it. And, while exhausting, educating others isn't always the worst thing. It can become a problem, when we realise what a lack of formal training might mean for us.

Will mental health teams challenge my gender identity?

A different problem, born too of the need to advocate for ourselves, is the fear of those who'd advocate against us. The media is quick to suggest a link between being a 'crazy maniac' and experiencing gender dysphoria – as a result of that, I have become very afraid of being honest about how bad my mental health is.

I personally suffer from some more unpleasant mental health disorders. While I don't feel comfortable saying much more than that, know that that discomfort extends beyond this chapter. It has taken me years to attempt to get over the idea that being honest could mean my HRT is stripped away from me. That I would lose all medical recognition of my gender identity in the face of a 'better explanation'.

How realistic were my worries? Well, for the most part I'm pleased to say they were unfounded. I've not had my medicine stripped from me yet, nor have I had my life's history dug into over nothing. But the fear itself has caused problems.

I had one particularly unpleasant experience with my GP. It was at the beginning of my attempts to seek true help. Before then, I had only been able to discuss my depression. Getting this far was a struggle, and needless to say, I was anxious. The conversation began innocently: pleasantries and a basic outline. Enough to ease my nerves a little.

I began discussing the nature of my mental health: delusions and hallucinations – beliefs that everyone who cared for me would try to hurt or kill me. As I went on through this, attempting to be honest, I was stopped.

'I feel like you're saying these things just to shock me.'

An innocent enough statement in isolation, but one that immediately triggered alarm bells in my head. Gender dysphoria – like other diagnoses – is primarily handled through the doctor's belief in the patient. If this doctor, one trained in advising on wellbeing, was willing to disbelieve me so blatantly, what else would they be willing to challenge?

I effectively shut down the conversation from there and urged us to finish up for the day. If I advocated too hard for my own legitimacy, would the doctor go on to critically examine other claims in my medical record? Try to form their own conclusion? It's not a risk I wanted to take. Nor is it a risk that the cis population needs to consider.

I got home, took some time to unwind and reported the incident the next day. I would go on to be given an apology for the unprofessional attitude presented to me. All well and good, but I feel the knock-on effect even still. Since this discussion, I've begun working with multiple other mental health teams. While none have given me this level of pause, I still attend each one with the fear that recommendations may be made to explain my identity as something other than gender dysphoria.

The strongest comfort I've experienced from all of this is learning just how detached the Gender Identity Clinic is from the rest of the NHS. It would take significant effort for anyone outside the network to advocate for my removal from the clinic.

However, that does by default mean there is one place where my fears are a lot more real: the Gender Identity Clinic itself.

The 'trans enough' test

Speak to any transgender person who has been through this process of evaluation, and you will hear the same story. There's a test of if you are 'trans enough' for treatment. It is conducted not in the hope of helping, but with the desire to catch you out. Going through this process even once is exhausting – but it must be performed twice at least.

The doctor with whom you need to be a perfect specimen of your 'chosen' gender will ask increasingly invasive questions: If you've ever been in a homosexual relationship, you suddenly need to prove that you're not a cis heterosexual. If you've ever had sex, you suddenly need to explain how that was possible - Surely, they propose, you must hate yourself to be transgender. Expressing sexuality is, for whatever reason, a sin during this process.

There are no touchpoints for how this interrogation is affecting your mental wellbeing. You will answer their questions, or you won't get treatment. You are expected to stomach your distress, all whilst talking about your traumas non-stop.

I was lucky enough to be able to be living openly as a woman by the time my initial appointment came around. While I have heard horror stories of friends being demeaned for wearing trousers and t-shirts to their appointments, I have always erred on the side of skirts and dresses. I avoided that part of the horror show. The rest, I experienced in full.

I don't conform to the typical 'feminine attitude': I am prone to swearing, I'm loud, I take up visual space. 'How can you call yourself a woman when you speak like that?' was a common question, both in life and in these interviews. The sex question came up, and, of course, the doctor in a sexual health clinic seemed to forget the existence of bisexuals and lesbians both.

Every explanation was countered with yet more questions, seemingly endless. A refusal to accept that perhaps I am simply a woman. This is their method: traumas are dug up and then blamed for who you are today. Perhaps being assaulted as a child is why you're this way. Perhaps that 'broke' you.

Eventually, you get to leave. You aren't told if they believe you. I didn't find out until I was asked to attend my second opinion meeting. It goes the same as the first: same level of scrutiny, same discomfort. You become aware that they have the notes from your first opinion meeting, and if you slip or say anything at all different, it will all be for naught.

But that, too, eventually ends. Once again, you are told nothing. After each of these meetings, I felt awful: the dredging up of traumas from the past, one after the other with no rest, took its toll. The supposed purpose of all these checks is to prevent people from accidentally identifying as transgender, but the true outcome is an intense fear of the impact of everything you dare say to these professionals.

And so, you learn to lie. Non-binary people learn to falsify a binary identity, knowing that entering the system as a non-binary person is a sure-fire way to be rejected before you set foot in the building. You learn not to talk about any doubts because a moment of weakness in your identity will destroy all your progress up until now. You learn to keep quiet about any mental health issues, even more so than in your typical medical appointments.

Unlike in standard healthcare where it would take some work and strings would need to be pulled to withdraw referrals, the doctors within the Gender Identity Clinic can withdraw their recommendation at any time 'in light of new information'.

I lived for a long time believing myself beyond the days of the evaluation process. The clinic was primarily about blood tests and questions about 'where do I want to go from here?' with the occasional life update on out-of-clinic activities (e.g. laser hair removal). That changed, however, when I learned that one of my professional opinions had been withdrawn.

It wasn't malicious, nor any 'genuine disbelief' – the person had simply left the service. Regardless of that, I was struck with severe panic over the matter. Knowing that I'd need to be reassessed, and that the interviewer would be reviewing my notes, I suddenly realised I would need to present the same information as I had 4-5 years ago. Sure, some details could change – but if they varied too much, what could that mean for my diagnosis?

I managed to get through my third opinion trial just fine. Given how far along I am in the process now, it was hard to really deny me on any grounds. It was deeply uncomfortable all the same, but I was – for the first time at any appointment – assured of the success of my claim. I can't express how much relief that made me feel. Still, there was a realisation that I was far from the only person at that clinic to have received an opinion from the now-absent member of staff.

How many others had to go through that process again? How many 'failed'?

I mean no exaggeration when I say that thinking about the process that I and others have had to go through to access a gender dysphoria diagnosis has kept me awake at night. Especially since I learned how easy it is for the opinions to fall away. The coronavirus pandemic has delayed access to healthcare across the board, but few services have a 'time-out' clause on referrals such as this.

It's hard to call this something we're used to – it's more something that we know we can survive. And visits to the Gender Clinic are rare enough that it stays that way. Still I would, without a doubt, call this the hardest part of the mental health system for me. And it's nearly universal to the trans experience.

Surviving the system

With those experiences put to paper, it is worth noting the positive parts. For starters, my ongoing psychiatric examinations haven't so much as touched on my gender identity. It is odd to celebrate a lack of discrimination, but I'm well aware that this would have been worse in the past. Sometimes, an absence is all we can really hope for.

I am very lucky to be dealing with these issues in the 2020s rather than the 2010s or earlier. Prior to the publication of the DSM-V in 2013, when 'gender dysphoria' was still 'gender identity disorder', it would have been a lot easier to write me off. The shift to defining gender identity not by an individual's 'wrong' mind but by their troubles has brought with it a greater understanding of the variety of what it means to be trans – which has in turn allowed more of us to access the correct treatment.

I do not take it for granted that my age means I have a smaller pool of negative experiences. Had I been born 10 years earlier, I can imagine writing a much worse account. I am blessed that the majority of my problems with the system have been based on misunderstandings and some of my culturally instilled fears have proved to be outdated. However, progress still needs to be made.

I find it disgusting that our policy towards access to a gender dysphoria diagnosis is still targeted towards helping protect cisgender people rather than assisting transgender applicants. Not only are cis applicants to the process a miniscule minority, but the side effect of these protections is severe mental anguish and uncertainty for tens of thousands of people nationwide. All due to a misguided fear that cisgender people may explore their identity wrong, all of which is entirely reversible.

Outside of the field of medicine directly, motions must be taken to cease using transgender people as antagonists in the media. The repeated portrayal of us as predators, abusers or inconsiderate monsters is sickening. Not only does it perpetuate the idea that transgender people are out to hurt you - it also instils a fear in us that if we are truthful about our struggle, we lose our chance at happiness.

We're just humans, wishing one day to be treated as such.

Growing up, my trans elders told me of trials to come, of what to expect, of what to fear - and that by the end I would be okay. I spoke with others, and we could bond over the mutual struggle. We've spoken to those just coming out and advised on how to get the treatment they deserve.

I have hope that we can see great changes in the next few years, but this means recognising where the problems lie. Not only in the medical system, but as a community and as a society. Until then, we have each other. Either through verbal retellings or written accounts, it's important to tell our stories. Knowing that the process is survivable is how we withstand what we do.

Nothing exists in a vacuum, and none of us are alone. We pass the torch and fight for that better world. We shouldn't have to be used to this.

ONLY WOMEN GET JILTED – Luke 'Luca' Cockayne

We buried the wedding dress on the hill, a few minutes' walk away from the observatory where you and I were supposed to marry. My girlfriend snapped pictures as I bent double with the shovel and threw dirt over the symbol of all I had lost. I looked ridiculous in that dress. Not that I'd been planning to marry you in it. I'd bought it after you left, specifically for this purpose. An artistic artifact, a physical metaphor. It disappeared under the leaves and soil and I felt lighter.

Only women get jilted. Have you ever heard of a man being jilted? No. It's all Miss Havisham growing old in tattered lace obsessed with the past. Like me, spending my time in memories, lingering on your face. Remembering that faded scar next to your nose. I forget the story behind it. Hurts that I'll never again hear you tell it.

***

This morning I rubbed three pea-sized dollops of testosterone gel into the skin below my belly button and thought of you.

I don't think you much liked me as a woman.

Do you remember making out in your bedroom, me in my binder and your t-shirt? You running your hands through my short hair. After you left, I cried because I never got to fuck you like we talked about, like I wanted to. I have no idea what happened to that strap-on dildo we had under the bed in our shared apartment with the raspberries growing in the garden.

I miss you.

***

I have no idea how to fit all these pieces together, even if I wanted to. That girlfriend who told me she loved me despite my trauma but never really saw the full extent of my hysteria like you did – she no longer speaks to me. She stopped around the time I came out as non-binary/trans masc – though it could just be a coincidence. A mutual friend told me it had nothing to do with that, but I know her and I suspect she hates the idea that she could have loved

Do I have a masculine soul?

***

Do you remember that drawing you did of the both of us? You were wearing the wedding dress and I was in smart trousers, arm around your shoulders if I recall correctly. You were leaning into me and smiling happily. What happened to us?

I should never have grown my hair long. Or at least I should have, I should have, I should have known.

I am so full of regret.

***

Being here, having access to black market hormone replacement therapy – friend of a friend of a friend on the internet – we are able to be who we want to be.

I look in the mirror and imagine my features becoming sharper, squarer, deeper, hairier. Imagine you beside me.

I will probably never see you again. And if I did, would you recognise me?

***

The psychiatric hospitals are often gendered. Men in this wing, women in the other. Where will I fit? Will I need to wear my binder day in, day out? My poor shoulder.

I don't want to be a woman anymore. I am so tired of trying to fit into that box. I want to wear trousers and slack off, be taken care of by the nurses who fuss and fuss over the men and leave the women to piss themselves alone and terrified in their rooms. We had to step up, look after each other.

Am I abandoning them? The other women?

Or will I be able to change hearts and minds if I infiltrate the men? Stand up for my sisters. But they wouldn't be my sisters anymore.

It makes my head hurt.

***

I set the table for you, but you didn't visit. You didn't call. I told people about my fiancé and they thought, they thought I made you up. A symptom of my psychosis. That's how unreachable and invisible you were.

Traces of you, traces of you haunt me still. A book on the theory of comics that you left behind. A mug from the artists' studio where you helped me run a stall. The first comic you ever made for my zine: it shows your alter-ego approaching a door, bucket in hand, the word ISSUES on the door. He opens the door and immediately slams it shut without entering. The word on it changes to MESSY. I have studied his confident initial stride so many times, the look of fear on his face as he leans against the closed door trying to contain what's within. Was it about me? Our relationship? Feminism and gender generally? Or just how out of your depth you felt by everything?

I try to not blame you for leaving.

A boy I like accused me the other day of being too binary, for someone who is non-binary. He said my loyalty still lies with women.

Obviously.

Though I am becoming more sympathetic to men's issues. I still feel like I wouldn't feel quite so ruined if maybe I'd transitioned before losing my mind, before pushing you to breaking point and beyond.

Would I still have been treated so badly in the hospitals? Especially the local one? I feel like the guys had it so easy compared to us. I was constantly being reprimanded for talking to the male patients, borrowing cigarettes from them and smiling. Being accused of flirting when all I was doing was flattering in an attempt to get a little nicotine.

The psychiatrist who tried to link everything back to the sexual assaults I was subjected to by that boyfriend I had at nineteen. Who whittled out of me that I'd had an online relationship with a woman in her thirties when I was fourteen. Who made me feel unclean. Used up. 'No wonder your fiancé left you, you're such a slut.'

And yet. Do you remember how I was stone before I met you? I'm sure I told you. All those years we lay side by side in your bed and never went further than making out. Until I cut my hair, I didn't want… I didn't want you seeing me as…

Across the photos of me in that ridiculous dress, I wrote, 'I could have been your wife'.

We both know I would have hated that.

Only women get jilted. I rub the testosterone into my lower belly and think about the possibility of running into you one day, of you not recognising me. New name, deep voice, it would take you a moment and then you'd see me and remember the person you used to love underneath all of that crazy.

Trans masc. Non-binary. The real me.

21

'CLINICAL ISSUE': HOW PATHOLOGISING TRANSNESS FORCES US BACK INTO THE CLOSET AND ENABLES ABUSE - EO (pen name)

It took me some time to process the fact that I was transgender. I was sixteen years old when I first came out, at the time I was a patient on a CAMHS psychiatric ward, and thus psychiatric professionals were some of the first authority figures I let see who I truly was. The way they handled my transness made an already turbulent time far more traumatic.

Late at night on the ward I was talking with a friend, who I'm still close with to this day, and it came out. She was supportive, and helped me build up the courage to tell a nurse; I chose to tell the one openly gay staff member on the ward. He was tentatively accepting but did not change his language.

The biggest problem came during my ward round that week. For anyone fortunate enough to never have experienced a ward round in a CAMHS psychiatric hospital, they are daunting meetings where upwards of five professionals (some of whom you've never spoken to directly and never will) all fix piercing eyes on you, holding up a vague pretense of listening to your pain whilst they impart the decisions they made about your treatment long before you had the chance to open your mouth.

So, it was in one of these meetings, sixteen and scared, I told them my secret; my request was simple: call me by my chosen name and use he/him pronouns. I wasn't asking for medical intervention, or even a gender identity clinic referral (I didn't see myself living the ludicrous number of years it takes to get to the top of one of those), but still I was told that I would need an assessment before I could be granted the basic respect afforded to my cisgender counterparts. Worse than just a no, I was told my gender was a 'clinical issue'; years later I still do not have the words for how crushing it is to be told that who you are is inherently pathological - that you are fundamentally sick, sick to your very core. Stubborn as ever, I protested, but it was futile; as is the way in psychiatric wards, the consultant's word is law and his edict was to be upheld.

Weeks passed on the ward and staff with a duty of care over me, staff I saw more than my own family, were unable to call me by my name. The impact was enormous; where I might have otherwise spoken to a trusted member of staff when in distress, I knew I'd only be deadnamed in the process and I couldn't face that, so I hurt myself more. Engaging in my therapy sessions became harder, because she couldn't see me for who I was either. My ward friends' support was invaluable through all of this. Violet and others from whom I've unfortunately drifted over the years regularly corrected the misgendering and deadnaming I endured and that really meant the world. I do wish to note that the ward staff were not at fault here, a few of them voiced to me that they were uncomfortable with misgendering me and almost all of them did switch their language smoothly once they were permitted. I was failed by my consultant, the management of the ward, and ultimately by psychiatry's insistence on pathologising trans existence.

When my assessment did come, it was one of the most humiliating things I have ever had to endure. I was sat down in front of my consultant and the ward manager (neither of whom had any background in trans healthcare) and they grilled me. I, a vulnerable sixteen-year-old, had to tell them how I felt about the most intimate parts of my body. I was asked to justify why I'd been seen participating when the girls had makeup sessions on the ward. I was asked all sorts of invasive questions; for the privilege of respect, I had to show them my most private pain. I'll reiterate that I was not asking for surgery or HRT - just for them to show me enough respect to believe me when I told them who I was and change their language accordingly. Whilst eventually the go ahead was given for staff to change their language, I should not have had to expose my most private pain in this way in order for them to believe me. As transgender people, we are the experts on ourselves, we are the experts on our own gender identity - not psychiatrists and nurses without an ounce of experience treating us or living our lives.

My coming out wasn't just turbulent on my treatment team's end; my mother also treated me incredibly poorly in the wake of the news. Despite the ward having some knowledge of what was going on, I received limited support in coping with what I now know was emotional abuse. In fact, my psychiatrist used it as an excuse not to bother treating the issues which had endangered my life long before coming out.

As a result of my mother's reaction, I was forced back into the closet for a year and a half. When I finally saw my community treatment team for the first time post-discharge I was back in the closet and far too scared to mention my gender identity in a clinical setting.

In the two years between my re-closeting and my eventual successful coming out, every letter I received from my psychiatrist listed 'ongoing gender fluidity' as a diagnosis. Not once did this psychiatrist bother to ask me about my transness - in his almighty wisdom he came to this conclusion all by himself.

Whilst this 'diagnosis' has now been removed, I remain deeply angry. The sheer audacity of it - to presume that you can know something so integral about a person without so much as mentioning your assessment of the situation to them is astounding to me. The fact that it didn't cross his mind that what appeared to be a change in my identity might have been a result of circumstances rather than pathology was a complete failure to provide me with either respect or care.

My experiences are sadly far from uncommon. When we treat trans identity as inherently pathological we necessarily leave the door open for abuse to be brushed off as 'reasonable concern', especially among young people who are already unwell and thus less likely to be able to identify abuse and more likely to lack the means to escape.

One need not spend long on a forum like Twitter or Mumsnet before encountering a parent triumphantly proclaiming that their beloved 'daughter' has finally 'embraced her sex' - a supposed victory for the poor parent over 'gender ideology'. Reading between the lines here, one sees an epidemic of young trans people having an integral part of themselves beaten (either physically or spiritually) back into the shadows. I ought to know, this is exactly what happened to me and the professionals with the duty of care did nothing to stop it.

Whilst many of us are lucky enough to be able to be ourselves later on, many will never get that chance. Psychiatric professionals have an obligation to intervene in cases of abuse but where transgender identity plays a role they are often either complicit or active participants. Young people who trust their parents and psychiatric professionals enough to show them something of themselves are being told they can't possibly know themselves, that they're simply sick, that their existence as transgender people is not okay.

These parents frame themselves as victims of their children's 'delusions', and use that artificial victimhood to bully their children into submission and clinicians who view transness as a 'clinical issue' all too often take the side of the abuser.

Whilst the World Health Organisation no longer views trans identity as a mental illness[10] - clinicians on the ground have been slow to catch up and the impact of this on the lives and psyches of young transgender people is devastating. Even if a trans person is fortunate enough to have a supportive family, if they're involved in the psychiatric system, they will almost certainly have an integral part of themself and how they experience the world pathologised - and I have experienced first-hand the damage this can do. To be told one is fundamentally sick, fundamentally broken, to have to bargain with individuals in charge of your care, and in inpatient settings and/or with the use of the Mental Health Act, your foreseeable future, can destroy your already lacking self-worth.

---

[10] World Health Organisation, "Gender incongruence and transgender health in the ICD", *WHO website*, https://www.who.int/standards/classifications/frequently-asked-questions/gender-incongruence-and-transgender-health-in-the-icd

In the 2021 census, just 0.5% of people in England and Wales said that their gender identity corresponded with their sex identified at birth, with a further 6% declining to answer the question[11]. Despite making up such a small slither of the population transgender people are significantly more likely to experience mental health problems than our cisgender counterparts. Stonewall's 2018 LGBT in Britain Health Report found that at the time of the study 67% of trans people had experienced depression in the last year and 46% of trans people had thought about ending their own lives in the last year[12].

Anecdotally I can tell you that we are grossly overrepresented in psychiatric hospitals - the first time I met other transgender people was during my first inpatient stay and in the four months I spent there the ward had at least four transgender patients. The way we treat transgender people within the psychiatric system is by no means a fringe issue - we are not going anywhere and we are significantly more likely to need psychiatric care than cisgender people.

Despite this fact the needs of transgender people with mental illness are rarely considered by either mainstream mental health advocacy or trans advocacy. Transgender people deserve respect, care, and protection from abuse as much as our cisgender counterparts and we are not receiving that from psychiatry; the way transgender people, especially transgender youth, are treated in psychiatric settings is not acceptable. This must change.

---

[11] Office for National Statistics, released 6 January 2023, *ONS website*, statistical bulletin,https://www.ons.gov.uk/peoplepopulationandcommunity/culturalidentity/genderidentity/bulletins/genderidentityenglandandwales/census2021

[12] Stonewall, "LGBT in Britain - Health Report", 2018

22

BEYOND THE BOUNDS OF THE BINARY - TOWARDS QUEER/TRANS/MAD LIBERATION
– Z'ev Faith

1.

For me, my queer identity and psychiatric abolitionist ideology are interchangeable and influence each other. Both require me to fight for liberation against state discipline and regulation of our bodies; to reject assimilation; to reclaim words that have been used to oppress and demean us and repurpose them into a sociopolitical identity, spit out recuperation. To smash social norms and the idea that normal exists. To live at odds with the world. And to subvert, disturb and dissent from the status quo, burning to the ground the idea that mainstream social respectability is something we should aspire to.

Queer and Mad liberation are inevitably tied up together; we can't have one without the other. And this benefits everybody; you don't have to be queer-identified or deemed Mad to benefit from the loosening of the binds of enforced gendered expectations and behavioural and experiential social norms.

Queer and Mad liberation means that we are all free to express and conceive our own ideas of who we are and who we want to be in the world without the crushing weight of restrictive cis-heterosexual and neurotypical norms and ideals.

My queerness, my madness, my transsexuality is not a disease. At times it can be extremely distressing to live in a body that doesn't feel like home and that cis-heterosexual society has imposed rigid and arbitrary expectations and norms upon.

To me, medical transition is not a curative solution to a medical problem - it is a liberating act of reclaiming bodily agency and pushing back against enforcing standardised gendered ideals. I love being the unexpected.

Being able to define my own conception of gender identity, my own inessential version of masculinity free from the restraints of imposed conditioning. My gender transition has allowed me to construct my own definition of gender without the constraints of coded gendered norms. I don't resonate with 'being born in the wrong body'. There is nothing wrong about my body. Like many neoliberal biomedical narratives of mental distress, that one individualises the problem. It disembodies gender alienation from the social context of the violence of being assigned gender at birth.

Mad and Queer/Trans liberation are tied up because I want to use my own words to describe my own narrative and experiences. I will not rely on an unbending narrative within the bounds of binary and segmented pathology.

Queer/Trans liberation means I have the freedom to present any gendered experience I desire and make use of all the things my body can do. Mad and Queer/Trans liberation give me the opportunity to birth my own conception of myself. How freeing it is that I get to decide and conceive my own image of myself boundlessly. I am becoming unconditioned. Nobody gets to define me but me.

My body is a site of pleasure, desire and social disruption. Distress is part of my narrative but I am not just 50% of trans youth suicide attempts. I am more than a narrative of pain and medical oppression and or the subject of hate and violence. I am mad – beautiful not because I suffer but because I desire. I am not a rigid, fixed set of organised sex characteristics: I am a multiplicity, an unbounded sacred and scarred body transforming and morphing within liminal space.

I emanate effeminate masculinity; I reclaim my agency. I reject assimilation in favour of degeneration and liberation.

2.

I was a freak from an early age, a precocious contrarian weirdo, a rough-and-tumble tomboy who liked to wear baggy t-shirts and tracksuits, play in the dirt and listen to Iron Maiden and Judas Priest while also having an obsessive crush on Legolas the androgynous Elf from Lord of The Rings. I was proud of my Otherness up until I wasn't.

The decline of my self-worth began through a process of psychiatric diagnosis. I was dragged to educational psychiatry and labelled with 'Dyspraxia' with 'Sensory Integration Dysfunction'. It is clear in the assessment that elements of these 'learning difficulties' are rooted in rigid gendered social norms.

The assessor criticises my handwriting as 'extremely messy and untidy for a **girl** of her age', which to me indicates far more about the gendered expectations imposed upon me than it does about my neurological structure.

By the time I was 13 or 14, I was out as bisexual and trying to crawl out of my skin in a desperate attempt to paradoxically destroy myself and survive my life. I drank heavily. I used drugs. I smoked. I starved myself, purged myself, crisscrossed a pocket knife into my wrists and burned myself by stubbing cigarettes out on my forearm. I hid behind thick blacked layers of kohl and ran around the streets of Camden seeking solace in the sub-cultural underground. I kissed girls and dated older men. I survived molestation and various other accounts of sexual violence including one by a neo-Nazi punk. I survived identity-based hate, standing an inch away from my friend as he was stabbed in the neck just because he was wearing make-up. I was desperate and distressed and made no attempts to disguise it.

I was ridiculed and shunned at school and my family didn't know what to do with me except react with contempt, fear and futile exertions to restrict my autonomy as much as possible. I wanted the whole world to know how profoundly I was suffering. I wanted my pain acknowledged. Instead I had an assemblage of authority figures who spent very little time trying to understand me but were quick to tell me there was something wrong with me. A CAMHS team, a psychiatrist, a CBT psychotherapist, an eating disorder specialist, a Jungian psychoanalyst, family therapy, occupational therapy, school counselling, special needs, extra English, extra Maths. I didn't feel like a person. Just a problem that needed fixing.

The more professionals attempted to 'cure' or 'curb' my emotional distress and behaviours, the more I resisted and made an identity out of this. My behaviours were a protest against all the injustices I had endured. They were how I communicated the unspeakable.

Unsurprisingly, it did not help to have countless authority figures reckon with me and dictate that there was something *wrong* with me. Never seeing me for who I was, or understanding where I was at or helping me make sense of what was happening to me. My already low self-esteem plummeted. After I had been diagnosed, analysed, chastised and blamed with no improvement, CAMHS decided on psychiatric drugging. And without much say in the matter, I was put on Prozac. I feared the person *They* were trying to turn me into. I became disconnected from my sense of self and blurred into the chaos and danger that surrounded me, increasingly agitated. Stillness was agony. I was trying simultaneously to make sense of and run away from trauma and abuse, and became fragmented and abstracted. My internal thoughts turned into inescapable hostile external voices that berated me and degraded me.

Upon sharing my unusual experience of voice-hearing with the psychiatrist, I was immediately put on the anti-psychotic drug Risperidone. Briefly the intensity of voices diminished, but with that so did my capacity to feel anything at all. I became cold, detached and dead inside. My movements slowed and I experienced extremely disturbing side effects particularly for someone who was already gender dysphoric. I developed hyperprolactinemia: my breasts swelled up to an E-cup oozing out a milky discharge. I was then switched to Seroquel and my Prozac was doubled. None of the side effects went away and instead, the volume of voices became ever louder, screeching, screaming, scraping in my psyche, binding me with no escape.

At night, unable to sleep, I paced, shaking, rocking back and forth. To be still was to die. I unraveled over a few weeks until I couldn't take it anymore and sliced myself up with a boxcutter and overdosed.

I drank the nasty charcoal while the nurse told me I was a 'waste of space' because I did this to myself and she'd rather be helping cancer patients. Then I was stitched up. I was repeatedly asked why I did what I did, but there was too much to tell and no words to express it. Besides it's not like anyone was *really* listening or to be trusted with the magnitude of my pain.

I was then abandoned by my family and discarded by society. I was incarcerated inside an adolescent psychiatric institution that functioned under the tyranny of surveillance, discipline and regulation. There were bars on my window. I was put on 1:1 observation, food and fluid charts, constant mental state reviews and risk assessments, given sleeping pills to knock me out at night. Every aspect of me was scrutinised and pathologised including my 'tomboy looks'. I had so little privacy and agency I developed a belief that they could read my thoughts and had control over my movements. Despite heavy monitoring, me and the other patients found ways and means to self-harm, drinking vodka and getting high. I felt far more driven to self-destruction than towards state-sanctioned 'recovery'.

Besides smashing myself to pieces was the most powerful resource I had for the obliteration of state property (my body).

After a few weeks, I was moved to a long-stay institution. While there, I witnessed and endured unspeakable horrors, abuse of Power, dehumanisation. I was trapped there for nine dull months and spent my 16th birthday institutionalised. When I got out, I was more traumatised and damaged than I had been when I went in. I resented psychiatry, and at the same time, I was stained by their words. Tainted by the sterilised, medicalised meaning they imposed upon my distress. The devalued identity of 'mentally ill' became an unshakeable aspect of how I perceived myself.

3.

Corroded by shame, failure, exile and marginalisation, I tried to survive a hostile world. I was consumed by a sweltering contempt towards my family for abandoning and rejecting me.

I spent the next few years falling deep into drug addiction, hanging around squats and drug dens that got raided by cops. I was raped by a drug dealer. I experienced drug-induced psychosis and would get so wasted, I'd be collapsed on the floor, eyes rolled back in my skull, foaming at the mouth. Despite the constant danger, the drug scene was the only place where it felt safe to be mad, but even there, I still managed to alienate people with bizarre and erratic behaviour.

I drifted through adult mental health services where I sought help that I couldn't get. What I did get I didn't want. I found myself on and off anti-depressants, in and out of ineffective individualistic psychotherapy. I sobbed in a psychiatrist's office, trying to express the aching longing to cease being perceived as a woman, to cease having to perform as a woman when I didn't want to or even know how to be one. I then refused a referral to the Gender Identity Clinic; given my experiences of coercion in psychiatry, I did not trust them and assumed they just wanted to force me into some sort of corrective treatment. It took a few more years of numbing out the pain with copious amounts of drugs and alcohol before I could dare admit how I felt inside. I lacked the knowledge to describe my relationship to gender.

My body never felt like it was mine.

Ketamine allowed me to exist dualistically, mind apart from bounded skin.

4.

I was 21 when I made the decision to come out publicly and move towards medical transitioning. I had reached a bitter end where the closet was suffocating me and I just couldn't stand to conceal myself and deny myself of my actuality any longer. The previous year I had already come out as non-binary using they/them pronouns, which paved the way for liberation from gendered expectations. But it wasn't enough to affirm my sense of who I am. It wasn't enough for me to simply negate womanhood and have a niche community refer to me as 'they' instead of 'she'.

A non-binary identity allowed me a sense of empty space in which I could then reconstruct myself. But things didn't get easier when I came out. My levels of distress increased as I was rawer than ever and acutely aware of just how it felt to walk around in a world that didn't recognise my perception of who I was. Each reference to my femininity was a knife in the chest. It was all-consuming and incredibly lonely. I felt a constant sense of both being overexposed and totally invisible.

My roommate at the time struggled with the name and pronoun change and wasn't particularly supportive. Once again I experienced family rejection; their reaction was fear, confusion and invalidation. Luckily, I lived 3000 miles away from home and was able to avoid much of the strain and strife by disengaging as much as possible.

The process of beginning my medical transition was arduous. I had to jump through several hoops and work my way through numerous gatekeeping professionals.

First up I had to receive a letter that confirmed my diagnosis, and I chose the route of Sexology. Instead of having an opportunity to really get to explore my gender identity and acknowledge any fears or doubts, I had to present myself in a certain self-assured way, hype up and perform stereotypical masculinity and conceal as much of my trauma and psychiatric history as I could. I got the letter but still struggled to find a doctor to prescribe hormones. Once I did find someone, he constantly used my mental state to deny me proper care.

As I was in a constant state of extreme distress, I was urged by those around me to 'seek help'. The psychiatrist I saw was hesitant to use my chosen name and when he barely had an opportunity to talk to me, decided my transgender identity was a manifestation of the *unstable identity* diagnostic criteria of 'Borderline Personality Disorder'. It is so reductive to view the fluidity of queer identity as a pathology. But all this conveys the limitations of the diagnostic gaze and how it is used as an oppressive tool to enforce cisgender/heterosexuality as a social norm. Meanwhile the anger I expressed at injustice was also conveniently dismissed and pathologised as 'inappropriate'. Under psychiatry, a marginalised person's response to their oppression is reduced to an individual pathology, which is then 'cured' through pervasive silencing - the subduing of our voices with hefty doses of psychotropics. The same psychiatrist also noted that I had a 'Transgenderism issue'. He went on to drug me with 14 different psychiatric drugs over a 2-year period.

I faced housing instability: my roommate's constant erasure of my identity wore me down. We fell out and she kicked me out. I then moved into a mad-friendly, queer-punk sanctuary 'Skidhaus.' A place where I could belong, express myself fully.

Yet on the streets I got beaten blue and bloody, further compounding the looming threat and background noise of transphobia, identity invalidation and gender dysphoria and the pain of family rejection. More and more I felt entombed by society's devaluing and incongruent perceptions of me and trapped in a dangerous world. The constant changing of psychiatric drugs and total lack of understanding didn't help matters either. In the general medical system, my psychiatric history was consistently weaponised against to me to gaslight me and undermine my treatment. In the psych system, my transsexual identity was utilised against me too. During one hospitalisation, a psych nurse tried to get me to do a urine sample. When I refused to comply because I was menstruating, she called a 'Code White' (aggressive behaviour) on me and coerced me to give a bloody-piss sample, humiliating and disgracing me in the process. I was then restrained, sedated and fell into a traumatic restless slumber.

Yet again I experienced lactation from anti-psychotics. I discontinued them but was stuck on the psychiatric drug carousel with an iatrogenic neurological injury. I tried to take my life, ending up in the ICU. I was sick of it all – all the medical injustices, the constant ridiculing, the daily misgendering every time I interacted with a human. The aching disempowerment. After a psychologist refused to sign a letter for top surgery, due to his own discomfort, I tried to take my life again and wound up chained in 5-point restraints to a psych-ward gurney. The hospital left me to decay in my putrid menstrual filth for hours, and refused to give me my hormones for six days. The mistreatment I faced in the medical system as a trans person was - and is - repeated and repeated.

***

When telling this tale of madness and transsexual transformation, I refuse to wrap the narrative up neatly. We all know that the sane and/or cisgender love a nice heartwarming story of triumph of the spirit where against all odds the protagonist overcomes adversity - but that's not who I am, or where I am at. I am not there yet, and I may never be. I am mad, I am messy and I still struggle with disempowerment and trying to survive in a world that doesn't want me in it. I am long-term disabled and chronically unemployable due to iatrogenic brain injury caused by years and years of psychiatric drugging. I am currently using a harm reduction method to taper off, and in the process, suffering debilitating withdrawal symptoms. Existing is for the most part an incredibly painful experience full of profound suffering. I am seven years into medically transitioning and have been on the Gender Identity Clinic waiting list for over four years, without an initial appointment. This denies me access to gender-affirming surgery. Meanwhile I have no doctor to help me balance my sky-high testosterone levels.

However, with all that said, I do want to offer the reader some semblance of hope. I have found my way out of the oppressive restraints of the psychiatric system that traumatised me and very well almost killed me. And I have found ways of understanding and making sense and meaning out of my mental distress and unusual experience within their spiritual / sociopolitical contexts, so that I don't rely on despotic reductive biomedical psychiatric ideology. This means I have the freedom to redefine who I am, who I want to be and how I express myself. I am four years clean and sober. I stay alive out of spite, and I will live to see the flame fueled by the rage inside of me burn down the systems of injustice that are harming instead of helping us - and with that, we can look after each other and create our own systems of care.

Feminism: An Aid to Understanding Personal Abuse in a Societal Context – Freida Blenkinslop

In this chapter I aim to name, explore, and hold to account the patriarchy in the shaping of my identity as a lesbian survivor of trauma and psychiatric abuse and as a life-long mental health service dodger.

Patriarchy did a really good job on me because still I hide. I hide my shame and self-blame for the things which have been done to me, and my fear of being "found out" as a survivor of physical, sexual, and psychiatric abuse which has me living in incapacitating shame – even though it was many years ago. I still struggle with the echoes of the past from day to day and fear it would cost me my job, which gives me a great sense of meaning, and other people's respect.

It would not have been possible for my family, or psychiatry, to get away with their abuses without the condoning, or at least lack of questioning, of wider society. The word patriarchy in itself is interesting and feels like I am setting myself up to be immediately dismissed as an angry militant lesbian (because this is what we do with women who speak truth to power), but my truth is that I am a still working on befriending the internalised hatred of most aspects of my identity and am far from the loud and proud people I feel envious of.

I remember vividly the first time I encountered the concept of patriarchy as a student, where suddenly the invisible was made visible and could never be unseen. At a conference in a place I'd never before seen the like of, from hundreds of students, four of us turned up to a women's group which had caught my attention. I mostly listened and what I heard gave words to things I had been thinking about and connections I had made in the past, but those discussions joined it all together in a coherent manner. I remember my heart racing and the internal grin as I realised there was a way to understand things that I previously hadn't been able to quite grasp, but through those women's words, I was able to view myself and my experience much more compassionately. It wasn't just me that was messed up, it was the system. It was such a relief to consider the possibility that it wasn't solely me that was to blame for my own suffering.

This meeting, and others like it, offered a framework through which I could understand my family and psychiatry and start to believe it wasn't just me who was mad and weak but I was part of a very dysfunctional system. It felt so affirming, non-judgmental, and it was great to share an understanding with others thinking about things in a different way. It was at this same conference that someone (a man, not someone from the women's group trying to "convert" me!!) suggested I might want to attend an LGBTQ+/curious group. I hadn't considered attending, but feeling it would be rude not to, I went along. An ice-breaker exercise involved drawing on a piece of flipchart paper and sharing something that most people didn't know about us. I wrote in really small writing *"I've been sectioned"* and felt my face flush and my heart pounding in my ears as I read it out to the small group, but the world didn't stop. No-one really asked me about it, but to be able to say it helped me feel less ashamed.

That conference was a formative moment in the development of my identity as I let myself entertain the possibility that I could be a lesbian rather than the asexual being I had frozen into as a consequence of my experiences. That and subsequent discussions about the cultural foundations of patriarchy, helped me frame psychiatry as an extension of the trauma I had suffered at the hands of my family. I recognised there was a common factor in many of my most painful experiences - men - and coupled with that, I had instilled this sense of responsibility that the abuse, the oppression, etc was my fault, that through my behaviour I was somehow inviting it and it was only through learning to conform that I could prevent or at least minimise the impact of it.

Personal origins of gendered self-hatred

I was born into a family headed by a man who hated women and definitely hated me. My dad was carrying unresolved trauma passed on by his own sadistic dad and I became the receptacle of his frustrations as he polarised me from my brother and sister as his dad had done to him. From as young as I remember, he beat me, told me I had been born bad, that I was the cause of everything which went wrong and the world would be much better without me in it and I believed him. I yearned for his love and approval in a way I never sought my mum's and felt overwhelmed with grief and self- hate knowing that I would never be good enough to deserve it.

Outside of my house I was a fearless bundle of disruption. As the new kid in junior school, I ate lead pencils whole (to prove my fearlessness?) and smirked when my name got put in "the black book" and didn't mind standing by the railings at playtime.

Teachers were stern and punishing reinforcing the idea that I was a bad kid who was disrespectful and out of control. They didn't seem at all curious about what might be going on at home or alarmed by how threatening my dad could be at times; I didn't care and didn't know there might be an alternative.

At one point, we lost all of our belongings literally overnight when we were made homeless and although we didn't tell anyone because were told not to, how could school not have noticed? Here I'm making the links between my survival adaptations necessitated by my dad's intolerance and violence and how that then set me up for negative reflections of myself in the wider world too, it was like a shit gathering snowball of annihilating beliefs about myself.

From a young age, I learned to reject and despise anything female about myself in my unconscious bid to make myself more acceptable to my dad, seeing myself through his eyes as weak and intolerable. As a tomboy, being mistaken for a boy by strangers made my face flush with pride. I really wanted to be a boy, hung out with the "naughty boys" gang at school and at some level believed I was a boy and felt accepted as one of the boys.

The blatant body betrayal of early puberty was devastating as I started to develop breasts and menstruate way before I was ready. The boys taunted and poked me and I felt rejected and different and so enraged at my body exposing my undeniable femaleness and everything which went with that.

I didn't want to associate myself with girls or women, I wanted it all to go away and I withdrew into myself with raging self-hatred at my core.

After I was rejected by my boy gang, I couldn't find my place anywhere. Now, this would be labelled gender dysphoria and in a different time and situation I would have gulped down the puberty blockers (not that they are easy to access, even now). But I can see that for me internalised misogyny was at the core of my dysphoria –it was in the folds of my being and no amount of surgery could have fixed that.

In secondary school, I targeted women teachers I perceived as weak and got lots of strong reactions and negative attention. Away from my dad, I had no respect for authority because I knew they weren't allowed to physically hurt me so what was there to fear, but I had no sense of my own edges and felt quite out of control. I was in speedy hyper vigilant mode, got myself into trouble a lot and couldn't submit to authority, and frustratingly for the angry headmaster, dissociated when directly confronted.

Whilst I got great satisfaction from reducing women teachers to tears, some of the male staff found me so offensive that they would vent their frustrations after class at break time - one of them was particularly vicious in his character assassinations. I do feel ashamed of some of the things I did back then and realise I must have been a complete nightmare to have in the classroom, but how could they not see how empty it all was for me, how I did not know how to trust or ask for help?

I soothed myself with pain from being young, but I started developing rituals around it from about aged 12. I went to the school nurse for dressings as I just couldn't contain the mess of it, as resourceful as I was.
There was no way to lie about it and whilst she started off sympathetically it didn't take her long to tell me how immature and attention-seeking I was being; how her precious time and dressings would be much better spent with a pupil who was 'genuinely' in need.

She kept saying that hopefully I would "grow up" soon. At which point I went back to my botched homemade dressings. At one point, my year head started to suspect that something was wrong, that I was more complicated than my behaviour apparently suggested. I was 'splitting' more - either out of control, or mute and dissociated. A social worker turned up at our house which didn't go down well at all. My dad told her to fuck off and she never came back.

As I got older, I realised I could end this mistake that I was and ease everyone else's discomfort and aged 13 I took the biggest overdose of my life but was never taken to A&E. Instead, my dad and brother laughed after I came to a few hours later after he got home from work and shoved me under a cold shower each time I threw up. At some point after this, I collapsed in on myself shutting the world out, unable to speak. I now realise that was quite a loud statement.

Many months later I was excluded from school after I succumbed to the hypnotic rhythm of my head banging on the desk and couldn't stop. After that I was admitted to an adolescent psychiatric unit onto which I had projected dreams of rescue, of escape, but it was far from that.

Looking back, I see that my dad did a thorough brain and body washing job on me, which the school system reinforced.

As I internalised those messages of being the source of all the badness and the world being better off without me in it, I magnified them, manifesting in raging self-hatred, self-harm, violent attempts to kill myself, and the enduring machine gun toting inner critic still pacing on high alert round my daily life today.

This was all I ever knew with my dad being very clear about the family hierarchy, he named it, described it explicitly, with my brother second only to him reinforcing his hatred and disrespect for our broken and emotionally absent mother. My brother could do no wrong and was treated totally differently and given a power, authority and sanctioned brutality in a way a child never should be. When he started to sexually abuse me, my overwhelming fear was of my dad finding out because I knew he would blame me.

Psychiatry's reinforcing of family abuse

I was kept in the psychiatric unit for 9 months, and during this time parental rights were removed from my mum and dad so the hospital could follow their idea of treatment without interference. I was routinely restrained by big men, which often included having my trousers pulled down so they could inject me with incapacitating doses of chlorpromazine. I was also put on bedrest for a significant period, forcibly stripped and put in a cold bath and force fed with a metal jaw clamp whilst being pinned on my back.

I was on "special observation" where one member of staff had to sign responsibility for me in hourly shifts where I had to be within arm's length and as someone who had learned to hide from very early on, this level of scrutiny, of being watched, really ramped up my alarm system as being seen in my family meant danger.

I knew that all I needed to do was comply and I would be able to talk my way out, but it took me months and many soul crushing experiences to develop the self-control to stop fighting.

I understand now that this was an innate survival response which had shown up in a similar way at school, not me making choices to fight against everything. I was taken in again under a section just after I turned 17 following a violent attempt to kill myself which led to me temporarily using a wheelchair for a time. I knew being taken back into hospital would be the consequence of failure so did everything I could to avoid it and to survive felt completely devastating. They kept me for a year and 3 months and unexpectedly let me go the day before my last tribunal was due to be heard (due to my solicitor saying a public enquiry would be a likely outcome). Back to my parents who I hadn't been allowed any contact with for over a year.

During these incarcerations, I was driven to the edges of what I knew myself to be. With the emotional pain of the things which had already happened to learning even with the promise of help, there was only more of the same. I had periods of confusion and disintegration where I had no concept of which way was up or what was happening. As it had done throughout childhood, my mind entertained me with its fluidity but with it the terrifying sense of freefall through boundless space. My experience in psychiatric hospital had a profound effect on me, reinforcing things I had learned in my family and school; that I was powerless at the same time as being completely out of control. Over and over again - primarily men in roles such as nurses, doctors, psychiatrists, and the police - used their power over me in ways which really weren't ok. It felt abusive and yet I felt responsible for it, absorbing messages that my treatment was of my own making and I just needed to make better choices. It reinforced the idea of the world being hostile and dangerous and that no-one with any power could be trusted. There were specific incidents that left me feeling broken.

I have become a trauma nerd, gathering all the information I can to better steer my own ship, but the impact of my earlier life experiences runs deep - most significantly in my relationships, or lack of relationships with others. I have yearned for a therapeutic co-pilot, a cheerleader on this perpetual journey, but get me in a room with a therapist and instantaneously my startle reflex turns up to maximum which is so visceral it's like my skin's peeled back. Simultaneously overwhelmed and dissociated, I feel like I lose control of my mind, and sometimes do. I once had a therapist threaten to call an ambulance after I lost myself in a session and more recently a therapist who terminated the therapy part way through a session saying it was too unsafe, that I was too complex (not because of self-harm or suicidal ideation, but because of the warpy places my mind goes to in times of stress) and suggesting I get myself a particular psychiatric diagnosis.

It's not like I haven't tried, I have really tried and I have yearned for a therapist to guide me towards hope and healing, but the reality is, vulnerability conjures up a storm which blows me completely off course where everything apart from the wild waves underneath me gets lost.

I have felt like a failure for not managing to heal more, for not being nominated for the trophy of triumph over adversity. I've definitely internalised the idea that I am to blame for my own struggles, for not being more healed, that it is clearly something wrong with me, something I am not doing right.

The narrative of shame and blame, that I've created my own victimisation (rooted in the structures of the patriarchy) and if only I would practice mindfulness, or take medication, or do this or do that, then I wouldn't suffer so much.

I have bought into these narratives at times with trips to the GP in search of a magic pill to take the pain away because it is real and incapacitating and hard to contain. My refusal to take medication or see a psychiatrist has provoked accusations of resistance, turning compassion into judgment and dismissal for my "choice" to "refuse help" adding another layer of realisation that I am alone in this, there is just me and there is no magic pill.

Discovering feminism along with falling in love and coming out as a lesbian gave me a sense of shared history of struggle and oppression which helped me feel like I was part of something bigger and helped my history feel less personal. Lesbian fiction, where love and struggle infused the pages, was like getting into a warm bath and I dreamed of those fictional women taking me into their arms and whispering reassurance and hope that things could get better. I found my tribe in the women's peace movement, lived at peace camps, supported other women at court and got involved in some high adrenalin acts of defiance which was my way of saying "fuck you!" to all that was wrong with the patriarchy and got arrested fairly frequently. I built my first bender and felt the liberation of housing myself and living how I wanted.

Reflections

Coming out as a lesbian was a combination of fortuitous chance (rooted in the student conference) and the embodiment of my political understanding. It offered hope of feeling less alien in that I could imagine myself as a sexual being in a way that I absolutely couldn't with men.
It felt like a sane and powerful choice and I'm guessing I may well have made different choices if I hadn't had such overwhelmingly negative encounters with men in my formative years. It's impossible….

These days, understanding and identifying with a sexuality is much less of a political decision and more about 'who you were born to be' but for me coming out as a lesbian was much more of a choice. We are defined by our experiences and I can't help but wonder if I had, had different experiences growing up surrounded by men who I have felt pushed to identify this way? It's impossible to know, but I do know my politics have had a fundamental impact on my identity. My way of understanding the world (with its systemic oppression of those who aren't privately educated straight white males) was borne of my childhood experiences. Feminist politics offered me a framework through which to understand those experiences in a way that felt less personal and persecutory and more like the system was designed this way and together in sisterhood, we could fight back. I felt empowered by the choices I made to live in a different way which culminated in withdrawing more and more from all that I found difficult. For about 15 years, I lived alone in beautiful out of the way places in structures I built myself where I could play freely with my madness overlooked only by nature which sometimes jeered and took the piss, but was mostly benevolent. I learned to be much less afraid of my own mind, found my edges and learned to trust the earth would hold me.

Even though, through age and time I get steadily further away from my early life, its apparently profound impact still dominates my daily existence the space it takes up, relative to my present, still dominates my existence. I don't dwell on difficult memories but I still haven't got a solid place of safety within myself to rest in difficult times and a core thread of my identity of being reluctantly alive remains.

Fragmentation has been my main form of survival and the older I get, the more fragmented I notice I have become which is both good and bad. There are super functional parts of me which allow me to do meaningful work well and there are the parts that hold the confusion, terror and distress which leave me feeling exhausted and perpetually on the edge of crisis in my personal life when I am not playing the role of a competent professional. It is confusing and leaves me with feelings of fraudulence and a fear of being "found out" - how can I be so competent during my day job and so utterly discombobulated in my own home.

These days I am less fearful of the wonky places my mind can take me and have learned the skills to keep navigating through until I hit calmer waters, but there is no doubt that I continue to be profoundly impacted by my early life.

I know that I am far from alone in my experience of this cycle of patriarchal induced trauma being compounded and reinforced by psychiatry. How our adaptive survival strategies are pathologised as different versions of fight, flight and freeze are drugged, restrained and forced to comply and how little seems to have really changed over the years.

Things have got worse in some ways with more agency staff on psych wards meaning that the central tools for healing complex trauma - humane relationships - are just not available even if staff cultures have improved in some ways. Hopefully expressions of distress via challenging behaviour in school arouses more curiosity amongst the staff and more emotional support *is* generally available, but problems are often still and most conveniently located in the child.

Giving their survival strategies psychiatric labels means we miss opportunities to offer children and young people some of what they might need to feel seen, heard, validated and understood, and hence offer relationships of refuge which are a great potential resource if offered early enough.

There is also lots of work being done in primary schools informing children that they have a right to live without being physically, emotionally and/or sexually abused, along with creating spaces and sharing tools to help them speak out, which we know emboldens some children to do so.

The #MeToo movement has been great for raising awareness about how widespread the sexual abuse and harassment of women is, along with its impact being compounded by the injustice inherent in the "justice" system. The Black Lives Matter movement has been building momentum for almost a decade, opposing police brutality and shining a light on institutional racism and the multitude of ways that manifests in people's lives. An element of shared experience survivors of psychiatric abuse have with these movements is that having personal encounters with these oppressions lifts the fog that most people walk around in so that everything is laid bare. Until you have a reason not to, most people believe the police will be helpful when you phone 999, that men are generally respectful and trustworthy and definitely that when a friend or family member is in distress, psychiatry has the necessary expertise to make them better.

ABOUT OUR CONTRIBUTORS

DOLLY SEN

I am a writer, speaker, artist, filmmaker, working class, queer, interested in disability & the madness that is given to us by the world. I am interested in this because I have been labelled mad, although I think my challenging of inequality and vicious systems of the 'normal' world makes perfect sense. I am interested in society's perception of mental health and madness – whether people think 'it's all in the head' and not a response to social and political issues. I My work has serious undertones but subvert things with mischief. In other words, I put normality over my lap and smack it naughty arse.
www.dollysen.com

JULIE MC

Please say the MACK, or you can just call me Mack, I loathe the name Julie and always have. I am told I write well. I have several useless awards doing nothing. Then there's one that made a very good doorstop, another good for chopping on and the most recent is great for feeding neighbours I don't want hanging round too long. I write because I have to write. It saves my sanity. Sometimes it helps me make sense of a desperate world that's been teetering on the brink of disaster since I was incubated in terror as an infant. I am an outsider, raised among outsiders. And that my friends, is a glorious freedom I have learnt to love. I'm a Disability activist and artist. I make mischief on stage, preferably theatres, but anywhere we gather together and throw light onto extraordinary stories will do. I am always seeking out new collaborators, wild minds who were born shaking up shit. If that sounds like you, do get in touch: www.intouch@juliemc.com

JAMES WITHEY

James Withey lives in Hove with his husband and emotionally damaged cat.

He lives with depression, anxiety and PTSD. He is a survivor of childhood sexual abuse, childhood grief, suicide attempts and anorexia. A whole load of crappy stuff.

He is the author/editor of six bestselling books about mental health and mental illness with Little, Brown. His books have been published in ten languages and in twelve different countries.

He is the author of *How to Tell Depression to Piss Off, How to Tell Anxiety to Sod Off, How to Get to Grips with Grief* and *How to Smash Stress*.

He's the co-editor of *The Recovery Letters* and *What I Do to Get Through*, published with Dr Olivia Sagan.

James is the founder of The Recovery Letters project which inspired the book. It publishes letters online addressed to people experiencing depression.
www.therecoveryletters.com

You can find James at:http://www.jameswithey.com
Twitter: @jameswwithey

JOHN-JAMES LAIDLOW [he/him]

is a mad, queer video artist living by the sea in Brighton, UK.

O.S (pen name)

I believe I am autistic, but I do not have a formal diagnosis and have pursed another one. I identify as non-binary. At the moment I am living outside the UK.

I would want to highlight that I decided to write this chapter and share it because it is important to bring attention to how people are treated.

I could mention that I sort out a diagnosis in the UK partially because I thought I would be taken more seriously – where I am based the mental health neurodiversity side of things is even worse.

I wasn't even able to get a diagnosis started here – each time I mentioned it, it was shut down.

LYDIA ROSE (@lydiarose_artist)

Lydia is a poet, writer and community artist from London, who labels herself a 'queer, intersectional ecofeminist'. She has an academic background in environmental science and politics, and a deep rage at the systemic violation of humanity and our shared home. Determined to live peacefully in a violent world, she channels her natural internal responses into truthful artistic expression and grassroots community activism.

Lydia loves challenging the capitalist heteropatriarchy by living as her authentic self; a joyful, playful, mischievous little fairy who adores cuddles, cute animals and subverting the status quo. She writes and performs poetry about all kinds of things that piss her off or bring her pleasure, organises events and facilitates workshops where everyone is free to express themselves authentically, and dotes over an awful lot of puppies, kittens, cubs and ducklings.

She also created Allie's Art Club (@alliesartclub), a grassroots community organisation that brings people together and supports their wellbeing through the arts, which she named after a childhood friend who's now an angel.

ARTEMISIA

Artemisia takes an interest in a variety of subjects from languages to sci fi and fantasy. She has a husband and a number of pets, all of whom are appropriately house-trained. As well as writing about her experiences with mental health and being a trans woman, she is also passionate about dismantling diet culture as a means to make eating disorder recovery more accessible.

RS

I am a naturally thoughtful person who loves nothing better than a critical deep dive into challenging topics, whether that is through conversation, research or increasingly through writing. Most of these thoughts are framed within issues of social justice, societal patterns and their resultant inter- and intra-personal relationships.

There is nothing I enjoy critiquing more than our mental health system, so the chance to explore gendered experience under the psychiatric system immediately grabbed me. However, it was my growing relationship with queerness which really excited me and immediately felt crucial to write about.

Assembling and editing this piece has been an amazing and difficult experience. It has given me the luxury to explore some fundamental parts of me, alongside my experience with madness and its treatment. The beauty of queerness, and of madness, is that they constantly evolve. The beauty of thinking, processing, writing and sharing is that it constantly flows.

It is incredibly special to be a part of this project, to be heard and to be held among so many other unknown, familiar and unfamiliar stories.

SOPHIE HOYLE

is an artist and writer whose practice relates personal experiences of being disabled, queer, non-binary and part of the SWANA (South-West Asian and North African) diaspora to wider forms of structural violence. Their work looks at the relation of the personal to (and as) political, individual and collective anxieties, and how alliances can be formed where different kinds of inequality and marginalisation intersect.

ALEX FARINES

I am a Brazilian-born creative practitioner and have been living in the north-east of England for the last seven years. I have had a difficult mental health journey and medical professionals could not always accurately explain what I was experiencing. My art has been my refuge in the darkest moments and acted therapeutically along with other coping strategies I developed to calm my body and mind.

GOBSCURE (sean burn)

writing as **burn**, performing-exhibiting-making-sound as **gobscure**, we use plural to reflect our broken-mind. currently artist in residence with NewBridge Project, previously artistic associates with Museum of Homelessness & Disability Arts Online (both lived experiences), self-taught, we playfully reclaim spaces for & with other marginalised folx. our solo show *heartfelt (*about hearts & heartlessness including our two heart-attacks as 'side-effects' of antipsychotic meds) tours this autumn.

ELLIE PAGE

Ellie Page is a queer & disabled self-taught artist, activist and an experienced mental health practitioner. She currently works across the North West supporting the development of artists who face significant barriers to the arts world. She has run an art 'lack-of-movement' in Manchester, under the moniker Still Ill OK, since 2018 and is cofounder of an intersectional digital studio, TRIAD³. She is a lived experience academic researcher of alternative & social approaches to psychosis and has been involved in relaunching the Hearing Voices Manchester. Her artwork has been exhibited in featured in magazines, and she has several publications. She loves Dolly Sen.

ARTIE CARDEN

Queer, Nonbinary and Multiply-Disabled Writer. They/them. I talk Gender, Sexuality, Disability and Media in general. You will probably find me reading, eating or crying over how cute my dog is. I wanted to be part of this amazing project because I love trash talking the corrupt systems in place in the UK, and the tiny spec of an idealist in me hopes it will do something to make a difference. Libra Sun, Libra Moon, Cancer Rising and a lot of Scorpio spattered about. You can find me across the internet yelling into the void about my commune dreams.
ArtieCarden.com

LJ COOPER (they/them)

is a Mad and neurodivergent white non-binary person, who lives on the Fife coast, in Scotland, with their partner and cat. They are a writer, artist, zine maker and researcher. When they aren't talking or thinking about zines, they can often be found riding their bike, making comics, drinking coffee or watching *Only Connect*.

HATTIE PORTER (they/them)

I'm Hattie, I'm a non-binary textiles artist and mental health campaigner from Bristol. I was diagnosed with autism as an adult having previously been misdiagnosed with borderline personality disorder as a teenager. I've been researching the high rates of personality disorder diagnosis in transgender people having noticed many trans and/or non-binary folk like myself having had similar experiences. I am a big lover of sharks, cats and fluffy blankets.

JO DOLL

Jo Doll is an artist with long term health conditions, they believe fiercely in challenging limiting policies within the organisations responsible for providing care and support. Often seen but not heard, Jo Doll uses their art practice to process trauma in the hope of illuminating the catharsis of creative expression.
To further explore Jo Doll's work, please
visit outsidein.org.uk/galleries/doll

ZACK MENNELL

zack mennell (they/them – born 1994, Essex) is an emerging (unemployed) artist using writing, photography and performance to explore queerness and neurodivergence in relation to presence and visibility. zack has been active as a performer, photographer and writer since 2015.

Artistic expression is, for zack, a way to make sense of the world and an attempt to contextualise who they are within it. In stepping into difficulty and pain through artmaking, they attempt to understand life through a different register to that of daily survival. zack wants their work to have an uncanny quality so that it might temporarily unsettle familiar places, making visible some of the strange aspects and tensions embedded there.

zack's experience of the mental health system has been convoluted and continues to be in flux, their difficulty navigating this alone informed their decision to contribute to *Birdsong from Inobservable Worlds*. zack's work reveals and constructs itself over periods of years, their contribution here is no exception. If their writing or work is of interest they welcome conversations and potential collaborations, their contact information is available on their website, www.zackmennell.com.

CAL

Cal was raised in Somerset, England but now lives in Glasgow. Despite living in Glasgow for over 10 years they haven't managed to pick up the accent (it is a source of great frustration). Cal exists within various queer and disabled communities which shape their outlook on life as well as their art practice.

Contributing to this book felt like a perfect opportunity to share their route through mental health services, and add their voice to the cry for better (or even just adequate) mental health and psychiatric care. Alongside writing, Cal has a visual arts and performance practice. They have exhibited work in Glasgow, Edinburgh, London and Newcastle and were one of the 31 performers selected for the UK-wide event 'We are Visible We are Invisible'.

KATHERINE MORISON

Katherine Morison (she/it) is a 23-year-old trans woman living in Glasgow, Scotland with an interest in collaborative storytelling and activism. As a disabled person on permanent incapacity, she works to use her experiences to inform further improvements to the systems we operate within.

LUKE 'LUCA' COCKAYNE

(he/they), formerly Ana Hine, is a transmasc conceptual artist and writer based in Glasgow. His work is highly autobiographical and has been published in a variety of forms including the anthology Naked Among Thistles, Artificial Womb feminist arts zine, DIVA, TYCI and others. He recently exhibited his paintings at the Pink Peacock café, performed at Turner Contemporary and produced a short play with Sanctuary Queer Arts called *Take Me To A Place Of Safety*. He is currently working on a book-length fragmented memoir with the working title *They Called Me A Banshee Cause I Wouldn't Stop Screaming Your Name*. His next exhibition *Funeral For My Deadname* at Saltspace Gallery will be a retrospective of sorts and will feature a live Deed Poll signing, as he says goodbye to his old name and the art he made under it.

His piece in *Birdsong*, 'Only Women Get Jilted' is a study in regret. It deals with his experiences in a psychiatric hospital and his fears about the system's gendered nature were he to become unwell again in the future; it is also about how he wishes he'd been able to come out as trans earlier in his life. He hopes it will provide some comfort to others in a similar position.

He likes Earl Gray with sweet almond milk and two spoonfuls of honey, or the bright pink Monster energy drinks.
@luckycockayne

E.O.

is a 21-year-old man from England. Following the events of this piece he experienced a brief further psychiatric admission in 2019, but has remained free from psychiatric wards ever since. He is currently studying for a degree in English Literature and is finally in the early stages of his medical transition after years of painful waiting. E.O. has previously written anonymously for UK based survivor led organisation Recovery in the Bin about his experience being detained under section 136 of the Mental Health Act and hopes to continue to find ways to ensure the voices and needs of Mad trans people are not left behind.

Z'EV FAITH

Jewish - Ba'al Teshuvah with a deep interest in mysticism and magic, a profound lover of Hashem, Torah and Talmud.
Mad – unmedicated, disorderless, a diagnostic dissenter after receiving over 14 reductive labels that do little to describe who I am or tell my story.

Queer as in an against the idea that normal exists, anti-assimilationist, a lover of those of the same gender and genders different to my own, queer as in undefinable. Transsexual.
Dis-abled/Crippled – the embodied experience of having a body that has been medicalised, a body that requires a mobility aid, the experience of living in a society that dis-ables me from partaking in it. **Feral Transsexual** – a hairy vicious T-wolfman who likes to bite, androgynous and not socially acceptable. **Psychiatric Survivor / Abolitionist** – Survivor of the violent mental health system, institutionalisation, diagnosis, overmedication, believer that psychiatry needs to be abolished and can't be reformed. **interdisciplinary Artist** – BFA in Studio Arts, a Manic Expressionist, an emotional exhibitionist, a performer, a painter, a screamer, a photographic creator, a conceptual dreamer, a noise maker. **Mad Scholar** – Creative Arts and Mental Health MSc, a survivor writer, experiential expert in psychiatric drug tapering, aspiring PhD candidate as an abolitionist researcher.

FREIDA BLENKINSLOP

I am a middle-aged woman continuing to try my best to steer my ship safely through these vast and hostile seas. My small regimented boat is brightened by cat companions and deep breaths on deck when the sun shines.

Navigation support with other survivors is the wind which powers my boat, my course set in the opposite direction to the squall of shame which frequently catches up and lashes down.

These years have taught me to hunker down with cats and supplies when the storm is overhead rather than constantly sliding around on deck adjusting ropes to try and change course. I have also learned to make the most of the sometimes fleeting sunshine and to allow my body to absorb the freedom evoked by the wind in my hair and sea mist on my skin. I still steer clear of passing ships (assuming raiding pirates) and am making peace with this lone journey I have chosen in order to keep my boat afloat.

THE CUCKOO'S NEST BOOK TEAM

PROJECT LEAD - DOLLY SEN

Dolly Sen is a disabled, working-class queer who has a brain of ill-repute that wants to disrupt systems that hurt people, not through trojan horse viruses but with my little ponies on acid with a little sadness in their hearts. Because of this she is a writer, artist, performer and filmmaker. Ten of her books have been published, she has written several chapters for academic publications, penned work for both theatre and film, and their subversive blogs around art, disability and humour for Disability Arts Online have a huge international following. She did some work in mental health archives and found only a small percentage was of the survivor voice so that's why she started this project.

Dolly currently resides in Norwich. She/They.
www.dollysen.com

EDITOR - DEBRA SHULKES (1975-2022)

Debra Shulkes was an editor and activist who struggled a bit with bios. She was a trauma survivor and a psych survivor: she can only write this because she's had the benefit of hearing and reading others' survival stories. Those stories filled her with words where there had been a hard silence.

Debra had been very lucky to have the chance to work on publications for the European Network of Users and Survivors of Psychiatry and the World Network of Users and Survivors of Psychiatry.

She had been trained in international human rights frameworks by psych survivors and disabled people. She loved supporting people to take back their experiences and stories from those who have framed and silenced them. She was part of (Re)-Imagining Mental Health Care, a Herstory memoir writing workshop for Mad-identified people.

EDITOR – DR CASSANDRA LOVELOCK

Cassandra (Cassie) Lovelock is a Black mixed race wheelchair user based in London. They are a writer, editor, speaker, and scholar activist who works and makes content across fields including mental health and neurodiversity, unpaid care, critical disability studies, and race studies. She has bounced around various universities including King's College London, public sector bodies including NHS England, and third sector organisations challenging traditional knowledge hierarchies and centring and platforming lived experience stories from communities who are traditionally ignored by those in power. She/They @ soapsub across the internet.

PRODUCER – CAROLINE CARDUS

Caroline Cardus is a visual artist and creative producer for disabled artists. She believes it is crucial for disability experiences to be part of mainstream arts culture, not just exist in a discrete, box ticking corner of life. In her art practice, Caroline makes work about the world disabled people live in. Through her work as a producer, she ensures disabled artists have a practical and creative ally to make bigger projects happen.

Caroline likes to work with Dolly because they both share a healthy belief in the power of the absurd – using subversion, mischief, and rage to reset false narratives of limits and disability, shame, and madness.

THANKS AND ACKNOWLEDGMENTS

DOLLY SEN: Firstly, the biggest thank you to my wonderful team: Debra Shulkes, Cassandra Lovelock and Caroline Cardus for their big hearts and big brains. Debra, your death broke our hearts, but I still wouldn't have changed a thing, because this was what you wanted to do, and so many of the writers felt your love, care, and mighty mind.

Gratitude to the people behind the scenes, like my partner Alison Rose; James Peto, Melanie Grant, Solomon Szekir-Papasavva, and David Cahill Roots of Wellcome Collection; Jo Verrent, Ellie Liddell-Crewe, and Cat Sheridan of Unlimited; and every Lambeth librarian and library that saved my soul as a broken and mad teenager by showing me books can save your soul.

Thank you to the non-humans of the project, especially Scamp the dog and Barry the Llama.

Thanks to Anna Sexton who inspired my interest in archives, and much appreciation to Robert Dellar, who kick started my journey as a proud mad activist.

Thanks to the reviewers and foreword writers who gave their time, and our indexer, Kate.

Big love to all the authors of the books for sharing truth and life, and denying the bullshit told about our lives. I hope you all see the beauty of yourselves.

CAROLINE CARDUS: Thank you first and foremost to all the writers, who bravely shared some of their most painful experiences with us so generously so this book could be written.

Thank you to my partner Simeon Every, and my Mum, Barbara Cardus, who gave comfort, counsel, and support through some very tough times, and to my cats Halo and Bella (collectively known as The Orange Anarchy Society) who freely gave snuggles and purrs any time they were needed.

Ever grateful thanks to our editor Cassie Lovelock, for being a rock - in fact, a diamond, joining our team as an editor and friend, bringing great wisdom, gentleness, and even more animal photos.

Thank you is not nearly enough of an accolade to our dear late editor, Debra Shulkes, who died in October 2022 after a short illness. Even after her unexpected diagnosis, Debra spent some of the time remaining to her in editing writer's manuscripts. I'll never forget your dedication and selflessness, Debra, and I'll never forget all the laughs we had in project meetings, just because you went on holiday and got Barry the llama alpaca (who went on to become our official project mascot) drunk on fermented apples.

Thank you to Debra's cousin Gail Sulkes, her friend Nicola Robinsonova, and Debra's many dear friends, who helped myself, Dolly, and Cassie visit Debra in Prague and in whose company, we mourned her death. You all showed us such solidarity, community, and friendship in the aftermath of D's death – something none of us will ever forget.

My incredulous thank yous and constant amazement to Dolly Sen for daring to propose this project, and having the fierce, loving heart to see it through no matter what.

It has taken everyone involved in the project all their strength of will to place something so incredibly rare and incredibly important – survivor voices, at the heart of mental health debate and practice.

Thank you lastly to the readers who see the value of this.

DR CASSANDRA LOVELOCK: Thanks to all our authors, to all those who invested the time in untangling their stories for us to share; it has been the privilege of my life to work with each and every one of you. You have all given me far more than I will ever be able to repay but I hope having your words memorialised in these books goes even a small way toward all the healing that is deserved.

To Dolly, Caroline, and our dearest Debra, I feel so lucky to have worked together and so happy I sent that random email asking if I could join the team. Dolly, you helped me find and use joy as a way of wading through life. Caroline, your constant support, softness and solid helping of disability wisdom has taught me so much. And Debra, dearest Debra, I miss you terribly but know that I did my best to do these books in our honour knowing they will never be as good as if we could have worked together on them till the end.

Never ending thanks to my partner Dante and my friends for listening to me talk endlessly about this process, supporting me as I have grown as an editor and very much as a person.

Lastly, as with everything I do, this is for you, Ciera. You were never alone in your madness though I know you felt it. I hope you can be comforted from all these voices screaming about the injustices. I will never stop screaming for you.

DEBRA SHULKES: She didn't give us a list of people to thank before she died, but we know she loved the authors of the books and working with them. She'd want to thank each and every one of them. She would have wanted to say thank you to the people she spent her last days with. She loved her dad. She loved so many people. She loved the animals in and around her life. Hopefully, Debra, this is a good enough thank you.

GLOSSARY

The definitions given are the ideals. We, the authors, fully understand and acknowledge how the majority of these definitions do not adequately explain the variation in experience of mental health conditions

UK MENTAL HEALTH SYSTEM-RELATED TERMS

CAMHS: Child and Adolescent Mental Health Services; CAMHS treat people primarily ages 18 and under

CMHT: Community mental health teams; CMHT provide treatment for people living with severe mental illness outside of hospital settings

CRHT: Crisis, or crisis resolution and intensive home treatment teams provide immediate acute support for someone in a mental health crisis who has not been admitted to hospital

CTO: Community treatment order; a tool used by clinicians to allow a person who has been detained in hospital to leave hospital and receive similar treatment in the community

DWP: Department for Works and Pensions; currently in control of the vast number of state welfare benefits including Employment Support Allowance, a means-tested disability benefit, and PIP (see below)

Forensic Services: Forensic mental health services specialise in the assessment, treatment, and risk management of people living with mental illness who are currently undergoing legal or court proceedings or are actively engaged in the criminal justice system.

IAPT: Improving Access to Psychological Therapies; The IPAT programme exists to provide people living with common mental disorders such as depression, anxiety or grief an easy way to receive therapies such as counselling or cognitive behavioural therapy. IAPT has recently been rebranded to NHS Talking Therapies.

Inpatient: A person who lives in hospital while receiving treatment

ITU, PICU: Psychiatric Intensive-Care Unit (PICU) or Intensive Therapy Units (ITU); specific wards in mental health hospitals which provide intensive assessment and treatment to those experiencing severe mental illness

Mental Health Act (1983): The first big piece of legislation which details people's rights in regard to treatment and assessment in hospital due to mental ill health

NICE: National Institute for Health and Care Excellence; NICE is a non-departmental government body that writes and publishes guidance for health and social care services on areas such as health technology, clinical practice and appropriate treatment methods and health promotion

PIP: Personal Independence Payment; PIP is a welfare benefit in the UK primarily for disabled people or those with long term health conditions.

OTHER IMPORTANT TERMS FOR UNDERSTANDING THE BOOKS

Ableism: Discrimination in favour of able-bodied people

Disableism: Discrimination against disabled people

AFAB: Assigned Female at Birth: when a person's gender identity is different from the female sex they were assigned at birth.

AMAB: Assigned Male at Birth: when the person's gender identity is different from the male sex they were assigned at birth.

ADHD: Attention Deficit Hyperactivity Disorder; a common neurodevelopmental disorder defined by disorganisation and problems prioritising, problems focusing and with multi-tasking, impulsiveness, and excessive activity.

Asexuality: Asexuality is the lack of sexual attraction to others, or low or absent interest in or desire for sexual activity.

Ace/Aro Spectrum: The range of experiences within Asexuality or Aromanticism.

Attachment theory: a psychological, evolutionary theory which describes how young children need to develop a relationship with a primary caregiver for 'normal/' social and emotional development. It explains the ways in which people that lack that secure attachment struggle into adulthood.

Autism: A lifelong developmental disorder defined by social communication and interaction challenges, over or under sensitivity to sounds, light, taste or touch, anxiety and meltdowns or shut downs, and special interests.

Body dysmorphia/Body Dysmorphic Disorder: A mental illness where a person experiences significant ongoing anxiety in relation to their appearance.

"BPD" construct: The argument that Borderline Personality Disorder is a political tool that psychiatry weaponises against particularly women who present as 'challenging' or 'manipulative.' Often these women have experienced significant trauma and/or are neurodivergent, but these experiences are ignored.

Cisgender: a person whose gender identity does match the one they were assigned at birth

Colourism: prejudice or discrimination against individuals based on their skin tone; typically, among people of the same ethnic or racialised group

Dyslexia: a specific neurobiological learning disability which presents as difficulties with accurate and/or fluent word recognition and by poor spelling and decoding abilities.

Equalities Act: The 2010 Equalities Act in the UK consolidated all previous anti-discrimination law. Its three major statutory instruments include: protecting discrimination in employment on grounds of religion or belief, sexual orientation and age - but includes gender, disability, pregnancy status, and race/ethnicity

Gender dysphoria: Intense discomfort and distress experienced by those whose gender identity differs from their sex assigned at birth

Intersectionality: the interconnected nature of social categorisations such as race, class, and gender. Intersectionality explains how an individual can experience multiple overlapping layers of oppression and discrimination based on their social categorisations.

Invisible disability: A disability, chronic illness, or long-term health condition that has no obvious external markers on the body, or the disabled person uses no adaptive equipment that is associated with disability such as wheelchair or walking stick

Intergenerational trauma: a concept which aims to explain how trauma can be 'transmitted' through generations - particularly in response to traumatic events

LGBTQIA+ phobia: A term used to encompass the fear or dislike of someone, based on prejudice or negative attitudes, beliefs or views about people who are or are perceived to be **L**esbian **G**ay **B**isexual **T**rans **Q**ueer **I**ntersex **A**sexual + with the plus meaning other identities that come under the LGBTQIA+ acronym

Neurodivergent: An umbrella term that refers to the diagnosable diversity of the human brain and cognition - it includes conditions such as ADHD, Autism, Dyslexia, and Tourette's syndrome

Non-binary: a person who identifies as a gender outside of 'man' or 'woman'

Misogyny: an ingrained or very strong prejudice against women

Misogynoir: a term used to show how sexism and racism manifest in black women's lives to create intersecting forms of oppression

Monogamous : the practice of having a single partner

Pansexual : a person who is attracted to people of all genders

POC: Abbreviation for people or person of colour, primarily used to describe any person who is not white.

Polyamorous (poly) : the practice of having multiple partners, all of whom are aware of and consent to the other relationships

Racism: prejudice and/or discriminatory treatment by an individual, community, or institution against a someone on the basis of their membership of a particular racial or ethnic group that is a minority or marginalised.

Racialisation: The process of the social construction of race; societies ascribe racial identities/social practices onto a group which did not identify itself in such a manner. Racialisation tends to arise from the dominant group ascribing a racial identity to a minority group for the purpose of othering and social exclusion.

Somatiser/Somatisation: Someone who presents with physical symptoms but have no biomarker or organic markers for the symptoms. Within mental illness, being labelled a somatiser often sees physical symptoms brushed off as 'all in your head' leading to struggles accessing support for physical needs.

Transgender : a person whose gender identity does not match the one they were assigned at birth

Transmisogyny: the intersection of transphobia and misogyny as experienced by trans women and transfem presenting people.

Transphobia: Originally Prejudice or discrimination against someone who is transgender. Now the term transphobia is used inclusive of violence and hate crime against someone who is not cisgender

With thanks to Cal and Cassie Lovelock

INDEX

ADHD (attention deficit hyperactivity disorder) 140, 145, 149, 152, 183, 188
Ahmed, Sara
    Queer Phenomenology: Orientations, Objects, Others 94
AIDS epidemic 102
alienation 50
'All in the Mind' radio programme 14
Allie's Art Club 253
alters 74, 76
angioedema 116
anorexia nervosa 86–91 *see also* eating disorders
anti-depressants 101, 183, 233
anti-psychiatry 101
anti-psychotic medication 101, 124, 231–2, 236
anxiety 13, 57–8
    GAD 174
Anxiety (Cal) 204*f*
Anzaldúa, Gloria 158
Apparently Normal Part of Personality 74
Artemisia 73–83, 254
arts, the 68–72, 119
asexuality 16, 17, 89, 92, 93, 147–8
asylum seekers 106
attention deficit hyperactivity disorder (ADHD) 140, 145, 149, 152, 183, 188
austerity 116
Autism 49–59, 140, 145, 183
aversion therapy 7, 14–16
    military, the 30

benefits 201–2
bi-erasure 116
binaries 158
binders 169*f*
biphobia 116, 119, 120

bipolar 186, 187 188 *see also* manic depression
Birdsong Collage 1 (Mennell, Zack) 190*f*
Birdsong Collage 2 (Mennell, Zack) 191*f*
Birdsong Collage 3 (Mennell, Zack) 192*f*
bisexuality 114–25, 129–31
Black Lives Matter movement 250
Blenkinslop, Freida 238–50, 261–2
body, the 82–3
body dysphoria 104
body image 103–5
borderlands 158
borderline personality disorder (BPD) *see* BPD
BPD (borderline personality disorder) 148–9, 155–6, 174
    diagnosis 103–5, 167
    Girl, Interrupted 187
    transgender people 165–7, 235
Brokeback Mountain (Lee, Ang) 129
Buffy the Vampire Slayer TV series 126
bullying 144, 230
burlesque 194, 202–3
Burn, Sean 113–25, 255

Cal 194–205*f,* 258
    Anxiety 204*f*
    Welcome Here 205*f*
Cameron, David 120
Carden, Artie 140–53, 256
care 91–3
care in the community 101–2
childbirth 179
childhood
    Doll, Jo 173, 176
    Faith, Z'ev 229–30
    Laidlow, John-James 43–4
    McNamara, Julie 24–8, 31
    Mennell, Zack 179
    OS 49
    Porter, Hattie 164

Rose, Lydia 64
Sen, Dolly 19–20
Clause 28 *see* Section 28
Clegg, Nick 120
clothing 27–8, 29
Cockayne, Luke 'Luca' 216–20, 259–60
cognitive behavioural therapy 188
coming out 22, 130, 146, 168, 1217 221–2, 223, 234
Community Care Act 101
compartmentalised treatment 95–107, 161
Complex Cases Service (Personality Disorder Pathway) 156
Complex-PTSD 99–101, 174, 194
compulsory heterosexuality 20–1
consciousness 76, 78
Conservative Party 120
consumerism 118
conversion therapy 15–16
Cooper, LJ 154–62, 256
coping methods 62–3, 109, 237
core 74
counselling 140–2, 145–6, 148–9, 152–3 *see also* therapy
    sexuality 176–7
crisis care 46, 184, 189, 197–8
cult abuse 63, 64–8

Dalai Lama 136–7
dating apps 105
DBT (Dialectical Behaviour Therapy) 156
deadnaming 222
depression 13, 226
desire 85, 87, 88–9, 91, 92–4
diagnosis 97–9, 149, 155–6, 229, 235
    BPD 164–5, 167
    EUPD 187, 188
    gender dysphoria 209–14
    lying 211

Diagnostic and Statistical Manual of Mental Disorders (DSM) 14, 122, 165, 213
Dialectical Behaviour Therapy (DBT) 156
DID (Dissociative Identity Disorder) 73–83
dignity 131
disabilities 116, 126–7
    benefits 201–2
disassociation 77, 134, 146, 242–3
disorder 74–7, 178
discrimination 13, 59, 99, 102, 213 *see also* homophobia *and* transphobia
Dissociative Identity Disorder (DID) 73–83
D'lish, Catherine 194
Doll, Jo 170–8, 257
domestic abuse 26–7, 28, 240–1, 244
drug addiction 233
DSM (Diagnostic and Statistical Manual of Mental Disorders) 14, 122, 165, 213
dyslexia 183
dyspraxia 183, 229

Early Intervention in Psychosis 156
eating disorders (EDs) 86–91, 96, 103–5, 142
editing 12
EDs (eating disorders) 86–91, 96, 103–5, 142
educational environments 142–4, 146, 147, 230
elder care 102, 107
electrocardiograms 184
EMDR (Eye Movement Desensitisation and Reprocessing) 65
emotion 160
Emotion Focus 170
emotional abuse 223–5
emotionally unstable personality disorder (EUPD) 148, 155–6, 186–7, 188
empathy, lack of 67, 134–6, 208–9, 220, 223–4, 243, 247
employment 116, 132
endometriosis 126–8

EO 221–6, 260
EUPD (emotionally unstable personality disorder) 148, 155, 186–7, 188
Everard, Sarah 66, 68
Eye Movement Desensitisation and Reprocessing (EMDR) 65

Faith, Z'ev 227–37, 260–1
Farines, Alex 108–11, 255
fear 37, 39, 134
feminism 238–50
fertility 128, 130, 174
Fisher, Carrie 189
fragmentation 249
Freud, Sigmund 124

GAD (Generalised Anxiety Disorder) 174
gatekeeping 16, 100
gender 49, 53, 58, 129, 146, 149, 154–5
    counselling 141
    hate 135
    My Transsexual Summer TV series 157
    psychiatry 149–50
    waiting lists 199, 201
gender dysphoria 82–3, 96, 104, 157, 174, 200, 241–2
    challenges to 208–10
    diagnosis 209–14
Gender Identity Clinic 16, 80, 103, 160, 209–10, 212–13 233, 237
gender non-conforming 19
    Laidlow, John-James 43
    McNamara, Julie 31
gender transition 78–83, 206–8, 216–20 *see also* transgender people
    evaluations 209–14, 222–4
    medical transition 80, 159–60, 228, 234–5, 234–5, 237
    medicalising 159, 161, 221–5

       name changing 80, 146, 160, 170–1, 221–2, 1234
       resources 161–2
       social transition 80
Generalised Anxiety Disorder (GAD) 174
Girl, Interrupted (Mangold, James) 187
gobscure 113–25, 255
Guardian 120
gynaecological medical conditions 126–8

hate 135
'Help the Normals' (Sen, Dolly) 7
helplines 61–2
heteronormativity 20–1
heterosexuality 20–1, 148
holism 96
homophobia 47, 116
       Cal 196–7
       Carden, Artie 144
       RS 89
       Sen, Dolly 21–2
       Withey, James 40, 41, 47
homosexuality 11, 14–15 *see also* homophobia *and* lesbianism
       Section 28 20, 120, 124, 125, 143, 155
hope 97
hormone replacement therapy (HRT) 216 218, 220, 235
hospital environments 133, 180–1, 220, 232
       admission 133–4
       assessments 45–6
       association time 29
       children's wards 43–5
       clothing 29
       crisis care 46, 184
       empathy, lack of 67, 134–6
       gendered 218
       humiliation 236
       mixed sex wards 134
       neglect 236 check other entry

        occupational therapy 37–8
        personality disorder wards 156
        privacy 45, 223
        psychiatric units/wards 221–2, 244–5, 249
        suicide watch 36–7
        transgender patient numbers 226
        ward rounds 221–2
hosts 74
Hoyle, Sophie 95–107, 255
HRT (hormone replacement therapy) 216, 218, 220, 235
Hunchback of Notre Dame, The (Dieterle, William) 30
hurt 41
hyperprolactinemia 231, 236
hysteria 11

ICD (International Classification of Diseases) 14, 165
identity 11, 13, 48, 79 *see also* transgender people
        DID 73–5
        fixing 157
        gender 208–10
        LGBTQAI+ 16–17, 105–6
        non-binary 49, 53, 116, 163–4, 198, 219, 234
        OS 49–50, 52–3, 55, 57
        self-labelling 81
inequalities 95 *see also* discrimination
insight 175
instability/stability 163–4, 168
institutionalisation 232
International Classification of Diseases (ICD) 14, 165

L Word, The TV series 159
Laidlow, John-James 43–8, 252
learning differences assessments 183, 229
Lesbian, Gay, Bisexual, Trans and Questioning or Queer,
                Asexual and Intersex plus (LGBTQAI+) *see*
        LGBTQAI+
lesbians 7, 14–15, 20, 22 30, 143, 196–7, 247–8
LGBT In Britain Health Report (Stonewall) 226

LGBTQAI+ (Lesbian, Gay, Bisexual, Trans and
Questioning or Queer, Asexual and Intersex
plus) *see also* homosexuality *and*
queerness *and* transgender people
- asexuality 16, 17, 89, 92, 93, 147–8
- bisexuality 114–25, 129–31
- definition 13
- lesbians 7, 14–15, 20, 22, 30, 143, 196–7, 247–8

liberalism 120

McNamara, Julie 24–35, 251
Mad liberation 227, 228
madness 11, 26, 28–9, 84, 86–7, 116, 157–8, 161, 227–8, 237 *see also* mental health conditions
- medicalised 159, 161–2
- resources 161–2

male violence 32
manic depression 189 *see also* bipolar
marriage 197–8, 216
masking 56
masturbation 180–1
medical records 10, 150
medical transition 80, 159–60, 228, 234–5, 234–5, 237
medication 101, 172, 231–2, 233, 235
- anti-depressants 101, 183, 233
- anti-psychotics 101, 124, 231–2, 236
- bipolar 188
- HRT 216, 218, 220, 235
- psychotropics 235
- sedatives 182
- side effects 124, 199, 231, 236
- steroids 127
- withdrawal 237

men 135 *see also* male violence
Mennell, Zack 179–92*f,* 257–8
- Birdsong Collage 1 190*f*
- Birdsong Collage 2 191*f*
- Birdsong Collage 3 192*f*

283

mental health conditions 95, 102–3 *see also* madness
mental health notes 10
mental health professionals 75–8, 109, 225, 230–1 *see also* hospital environments *and* psychiatry
    agency staff 249
    Autism assessment 50–9
    bisexuality 122, 124–5
    coercion 233
    crisis care 46, 184, 189, 197–8
    deadnaming 222
    DID 74
    empathy, lack of 67, 134–6, 220, 223-4
    gatekeeping 16, 100
    hate 135
    homophobia 22–3, 40–1, 89, 196–7
    judgement 176–7
    medical records 10
    misgendering 221–2
    neglect 223
    prejudice 99
    professional boundaries 33–5
    trust 195–6
    untrained 207–8
    ward rounds 221–2
mentality
    from outside 87–91
    from within 86–7
#MeToo movement 250
military, the 30
misgendering 221–2
misogyny 198–9, 240–2
mixed sex wards 134
modern slavery 65–6
Morison, Katie 206–15, 259
MPD (Multiple Personality Disorder) 74–83
Multiple Personality Disorder (MPD) 74–83
multiple systems 73–5
My Transsexual Summer TV series 157

name changing 67, 80, 146, 160, 170–1, 221–2, 234 *see also* pen names
Naylor, Liz 7–8
neurodiversity 158
    ADHD 140, 145, 149, 152, 183, 188
    Autism 49–59, 140, 145, 183
    medicalised 159
NHS 140 *see also* hospital environments
    administration 171
    assessments 187, 187
    bisexuality 130–1
    communication 184, 185
    community and care 101–2
    Complex Cases Service (Personality Disorder Pathway) 156
    counselling 140–2, 148–9, 152–3
    crisis care 46, 184, 189, 197–8
    diagnosis 97–9
    Early Intervention in Psychosis 156
    EDs 104
    fertility 130
    funding cuts 96, 101, 106–7
    gatekeeping 16, 100
    Gender Identity Clinic 16, 80, 103, 160, 209–10, 212–13 233, 237
    jargon 175
    medical records 10, 150
    misogyny 198–9
    peer support workers 157
    personality disorder wards 156
    PTSD 99–101
    trans healthcare 200–1
    transgender care 103
    waiting lists 63–4, 100, 104, 175, 181, 183–4, 188, 199, 201, 206, 237
non-binary identities 49, 53, 116, 163–4, 198, 219, 234
normalisation 7–8

One Flew Over the Cuckoo's Nest (Forman, Miloš) 39
online spaces 105, 114
oppositional defiance disorder 122
oppression 122, 165–6, 235
OS 49–59, 252–3

Page, Ellie 126–37, 256
panic attacks 61–2
pansexuality 200
pathologisation 13–14
patriarchy, the 238–9, 240
peer support workers 156
pen names 12
people 74
personalities 78
Personality Disorder Pathway 156
personality disorders 75–6, 108–9 *see also* BPD
    EUPD 148, 155, 186–7, 188
    MPD 74–83
politics 120, 125, 248
polyamory 196
pornography laws 120
Porter, Hattie 163–9, 257
Post Traumatic Stress Disorder (PTSD) 99–101, 174
poverty 116
power 40, 122, 244–5
prejudice 31–2, 99, 102, 104, 105, 164 *see also* stigma
privacy 150, 195, 223
professional boundaries 32–5
pronouns 147, 149, 172, 221
psychiatry 7–9, 11, 13–14, 16–17, 159–60, 249–50 *see also* mental health professionals
    anti-psychiatry 101
    bias 167
    birth/childhood 179
    bisexuality 122, 124–5
    BPD 166–7

    educational 229
    empathy, lack of 134–6, 220
    gatekeeping role 16
    gender 149–50
    hate 135
    homophobia 40–1, 89
    limitations 236
    Mennell, Zack 181–2
    oppression 235
    RS 88–90
    transcultural 105–6
    transgender people 166–7
psychosis 108–11, 132, 201, 231
psychotropics 235
PTSD (Post Traumatic Stress Disorder) 99–101, 174

Quant, Cara 30
Queer liberation 227, 228
Queer Phenomenology: Orientations, Objects, Others (Ahmed, Sara) 94
Queerness (Queer) 14, 15–17
    abuse 31–2
    Anzaldúa, Gloria 158
    Carden, Artie 143–4, 145, 146, 147, 150–1
    consumerism 118
    longings 84–94
    Porter, Hattie 164, 168
    RS 84–94
    tender queering 93–4

race 11
reality 77–8, 126
recovery 89, 158
Recovery Letters Project 252
refugees 106
rejection 102, 104, 119, 144–5, 233, 234
religion 111, 113
reproduction 127–8, 130, 161, 174, 197–8

restraint 8, 244
Rose, Lydia 60–72, 253
    Small but Mighty 71
RS 84–94, 254–5
Russo, Jasna 8

school environments 43, 113, 124, 142–4, 155, 230, 241–2, 250
Section 28 (Local Government Act 1988) 20, 120, 124, 125, 143, 155
sectioning 28–9, 239, 245
sedatives 182
self-care 60
self-esteem 231
self-harm 13, 140, 142, 144, 151, 156, 230, 232, 243
    LGBTQAI+ people 102
self-image 163
self-labelling 81
self-worth 229
Sen, Dolly 19–23, 251
    'Help the Normals' 7
Sensory Integration Dysfunction 229
service user movements 158
sex drive 199
sex education 143
sexual abuse 68, 220, 244
sexual health 89, 127–8
sexual offences 66, 68
sexual violence 230
sexuality *see also* homosexuality
    asexuality 16, 17, 89, 92, 93, 147–8
    bisexuality 114–25, 129–31
    Cal 196
    Carden, Artie 141
    Cooper, LJ 155
    counselling 176–7
    Doll, Jo 176–7
    heterosexuality 20–1, 148

lesbians 7, 14–15, 20, 22, 30, 143, 196–7
Mennell, Zack 182
Page, Ellie 129–31
pansexuality 200
polyamory 196
Rose, Lydia 66
RS 85–6, 87
Sen, Dolly 19–23
transgender people 210–13
shame 11, 15, 132, 245, 246
Skins TV series 143
slavery 65–6
Small but Mighty (Rose, Lydia) 71
social media 105
social transition 80
society 152
sociocultural norms 105–6, 167, 227, 228, 229
special interest band 118
spirituality 111
stability/instability 163–4, 168
state violence 102
statistics 151–2, 226
stereotypes 46
stigma 166 *see also* prejudice
Still Ill OK 256
Stonewall
    LGBT In Britain Health Report 226
stress 127
suicidal feelings 226
    LGBTQAI+ people 13, 102
    Withey, James 36–7, 38
suicide attempts 13, 151, 229
    Blenkinslop, Freida 243–5
    Carden, Artie 142, 144
    Faith, Z'ev 231, 236
    McNamara, Julie 28
    Morison, Katie 207
    Page, Ellie 131

support 63–5, 96, 125
    school 250
    helplines 61–2
supported living 47
survival techniques 68–72
survivor stories 10, 11–12 *see also under individual names of survivors*
    service user movements 158
systems 76–7

Thatcher, Margaret 124
therapy *see also* counselling
    aversion 7, 14–16, 30
    cognitive behavioural 188
    conversion 16
    DBT 156
    DID 81
    EMDR 65
    Emotion Focus 170
    Mennell, Zack 186, 188
    Rose, Lydia 64–5
    Blenkinslop, Freida 246
    RS 92
    talking 141, 148, 175, 188
    untrained therapists 207–8
trafficking 63, 66–7
Trans liberation 228
transcultural psychiatry 105
transgender people 16, 103, 104, 116, 150–1, 157, 164–7
    see also gender transition *and* transphobia
    BPD 165–7
    evaluations 209–14, 222–4
    expectations of 206
    healthcare 200–1
    medicalisation 221–5
    as mental illness 103, 165–6, 225
    numbers 226
    sexuality 210, 211

transphobia 19, 116, 214, 235–6
trauma 76–7, 100–1, 246, 249 *see also* PTSD
treatment pathways 96
TRIAD 256

Unlimited 10, 11

validity 79–80, 151–2
violence 114, 236
    domestic 26–7, 28
    male 32
    sexual 230
    state 102
visibility 99, 126, 134, 136
Viva La Vulva movement 30
voice hearing 108–11, 132, 231

Welcome Here (Cal) 205*f*
Wellcome Collection 10
Whatever happened to Baby Jane? (Aldrich, Robert) 29
Withey, James 36–42, 252
Wizard of Oz, The (Fleming, Victor) 40
women 1-2
    Autism 57
    BPD 164–5
    jilting 216
World Health Organisation 225

ALSO FROM CUCKOOS NEST BOOKS

www.cuckoosnestbooks.co.uk